7
4/21
SS

In Life, First You Kick Ass

Reflections on the 1985 Bears and Wisdom from Da Coach

MIKE DITKA

WITH RICK TELANDER

www.SportsPublishingLLC.com

ISBN: 1-58261-977-8

Publishers: Peter L. Bannon and Joseph J. Bannon Sr.
Senior managing editor: Susan M. Moyer
Developmental editor: Noah Amstadter
Art director: K. Jeffrey Higgerson
Dust jacket design: Kenneth J. O'Brien
Project managers: Greg Hickman and Kathryn R. Holleman
Photo editor: Erin Linden-Levy
Media and promotions managers: Courtney Hainline (regional),
        Randy Fouts (national), Maurey Williamson (print)

Printed in the United States of America

Sports Publishing L.L.C.
804 North Neil Street
Champaign, IL 61820

Phone: 1-877-424-2665
Fax: 217-363-2073
www.SportsPublishingLLC.com

To those men on the field who made this all happen,
and to the memory of the Old Man.
—M.D.

To the good life.
—R.T.

CONTENTS

ACKNOWLEDGMENTS

I want to thank all of those writers who documented the Bears' run to the Super Bowl, particularly the columnists and beat reporters for the *Chicago Sun-Times*, whose old news clips were so valuable in my research.

I also got insight and information from these books: *Halas by Halas*, by George Halas and Arthur Veysey; *Ditka: An Autobiography*, by Mike Ditka and Don Pierson; *Papa Bear*, by Jeff Davis; *It's Been A Pleasure: The Jim Finks Story*, by seven various writers; *Ditka* by Armen Keteyian, *Singletary on Singletary*, by Mike Singletary and Jerry Jenkins; and *McMahon*, by Jim McMahon and Bob Verdi.

Agent Steve Mandell and editor Noah Amstadter were incredibly helpful in assisting Mike Ditka and me in putting everything together. This book could not have been completed without the efforts of Susan Moyer, Greg Hickman, Kayte Holleman, and Kenneth O'Brien at Sports Publishing. And the Bears' old media guides, gathering dust on my office shelf, provided sudden and unexpected insights, such as the knowledge that after the Dallas rout Steve Fuller received a "gold-plated game ball" from Ditka himself.

When I floated the title for this book by Da Coach, he pondered it and said, "Well, it's true, isn't it?" It is.

He thought further and asked, "Think we'll sell many in Christian bookstores?"

If they stock them, I certainly hope so. As I recall from the Bible, a gentleman named Jesus did some serious ass-kicking upon occasion.

In life, first things first.

—RICK TELANDER

INTRODUCTION

To me, it seems like only yesterday that the Mike Ditka Bears ruled the earth. Part of that is because during the amazing and amusing 1985 season, I lived next door to the team. The east property line of my yard was the west end line for the Bears' practice facility at old Halas Hall in Lake Forest. A chain-link fence—with a number of large, rusty-edged, human-sized holes in it—a few ash trees, and some accidental buckthorn sprouts, were all that separated my house from the gridiron.

My wife and I and our two baby girls had moved from a two-bedroom Evanston apartment in 1984, risking everything I had on a down payment and a strangling mortgage, heading farther north in the 'burbs where things were cheaper and we could afford—strange as it may seem now with current real estate prices in this area—our first house. The 100-yard grass field next door was vacant when we arrived in the spring of 1984. It was called Farwell Field, I learned, and belonged to Lake Forest College. Remarkably, the Bears shared the field all late summer and fall with the mighty Division III Lake Forest Foresters, a band of cheerful, red-and-black-clad, non-scholarship collegians about the size of average high school players. The Foresters would tear up the field on Saturday afternoons against Beloit and Lawrence—really destroy the sod when they played in the occasional monsoon—and then the Bears would practice on the maimed surface the rest of the week. By late November the grass would be brown, clotted, and basically demolished. At the east end of the field was the low brick structure known as Halas Hall, with the large office window to the far south being that of young team president Michael McCaskey, and the window to the north being that of young head coach Mike Ditka. In time I would realize that as I stood in our ground floor bathroom when the leaves were gone, casually relieving myself, I could see into the working quarters of each man.

Of course, I didn't know much about this yet. I worked for *Sports Illustrated* at the time, and I loved sports. But mostly I traveled for my stories. To Washington and San Francisco and Pittsburgh, places where they had real NFL teams and real heroes. I had heard the Bears lived next door to our new place, but my mom had actually found the house and told me about it while my family was vacationing in Florida, and I made the earnest money payment sight-unseen. At any rate, in May when our burgeoning troupe—soon to be six of us—moved our few possessions into the old house on Illinois Road, nobody was in the big yard next door.

Who cared about the Bears, anyway?

The year before they had finished 8-8. Whoop-di-doo.

In 1982, a strike-shortened misfire, they had gone 3-6. The year before that, 6-10. The year before that, 7-9. You threw in with the Bears at your own risk. They hadn't won anything since 1963, three years before the Super Bowl was invented.

Still, the Bears had this fellow named Payton. And they had a nostalgia-laden tradition. And starting in 1982 they had a new coach with fire in his eyes, a sometimes-frightening, loose-bolt former All-Pro tight end by the name of Mike Ditka. He had replaced Neill Armstrong, coming straight from a special teams job with the Dallas Cowboys, apparently at old man George Halas's request. Which made folks wonder if the acerbic, grumpy Papa Bear had finally gone around the bend. Special teams coaches didn't become head coaches. Offensive coordinators did. Defensive coordinators did. Special teams coaches became not much of anything.

Ditka was a guy who broke racquets in rage when he played racquetball against Cowboys staff members like Dan Reeves and the great calm one himself, Tom Landry. Ditka made his Cowboys receivers run, and when they didn't run right, he swore at them. He challenged them to fight. Right there, on the spot, punk! He turned red. He turned purple. As an athlete he had been overwhelming in high school, dominant at Pitt, ferocious in the NFL. In 1983, his second year leading the Bears, he had been so infuriated after a loss, he punched a filing cabinet with his right hand, breaking a bone in the process. At the next game he inspired his team by saying, "Win one for Lefty." He was perpetually agitated, outspoken, a puffing volcano always on the verge of eruption. This was the head coach of the storied Chicago franchise, the granddaddy of the league? Help.

But, then, Ditka had been a *Bear.* For six years, starting in 1961, he had played like a maniac, on and off the field. He defined toughness and grit at the tight end position. Despite his Pennsylvania steel town roots and accent, he came to embody the soul of the black-and-blue division Bears along with two other disparate, striving souls—Gayle Sayers and Dick Butkus. Traded to the Eagles in 1967 and to the Cowboys in 1969, Ditka played in two Super Bowls and then was an assistant coach in two others. The idea of Ditka as a head coach seemed—what would you call it?—intriguing? What if his passion could be harnessed, focused, reproduced, and transferred like magic capes to all those scattered beings under him? What if. . . .

Nah.

Gradually the Bears began to make their presence known next door. There was a minicamp or two. And sometimes I would see Ditka in a golf cart on the edge of the grass, observing, gesturing, sometimes seated with oddball young quarterback Jim McMahon or even with the great, squirming Walter Payton himself. Sometimes I could hear Ditka yell. Sometimes I could see his orange or blue sweatshirt glinting through the bushes as he limped from drill to drill. He chewed gum constantly, as though his jaw had to move nonstop to compensate for the uncertainty of his football-ravaged leg joints. There were the usual practice noises—grunts, whistles, hollerings, pads cracking, the leathery thud of punts departing Dave Finzer's and later Maury Buford's foot and the four- or five-second delay before a reciprocating thud was heard as each ball touched earth.

Sometimes I would stand next to the fence and watch wide receiver Willie Gault sprint effortlessly after seemingly far-overthrown passes from McMahon and gracefully pull them in. Sometimes I'd watch the boring recognition drills conducted for the defensive unit by the taciturn Buddy Ryan. At the end of certain practices the Bears would work on their two-minute drill—a loud, frantic blend of chaos and creativity that often ended with kicker Bob Thomas drilling a hurried field goal that would arch over the antique goalpost at our end, soar above the chicken wire that hung uselessly from rusting poles above the fence and bounce off the roof of my house.

Some of those balls the Bears managers were able to find. Some stayed in my yard for, well … let's just say a few of them still haven't been returned.

I ran into Ditka a few times, sometimes after practices when I'd simply walk through a hole in the fence and have a chat with a player like Payton or Gary Fencik or, in years to come, a new draftee like quarterback Jim Harbaugh. Indeed, it was Harbaugh who looked at my house and asked if I'd be willing to sell it. "Man, I could wake up, walk across the field, and be there for the meetings in two minutes," Harbaugh would say wistfully. I pondered a deal. Maybe I could gouge the first-round pick. But where would we move?

Like most writers, I didn't get too close to the head coach. Ditka was intimidating. He was in his mid-40s and except for the bad-hip, bad-foot hobble, looked like he could catch and crush the typical journalist with one paw. I have a photo of him holding my third baby, Robin, in his arms in 1988, tickling her under the chin, seated in the empty wooden bleachers next to the field. He was always civil enough, and always ready to sign autograph hounds' souvenirs, but he was…Ditka.

"We call him 'Sybil,'" Jim McMahon would write in his biography, *McMahon*, "after the girl in that movie. You know, the one who had all those different personalities? Mike will be calm one minute, then throw a clipboard the next. People don't understand that, but we do. The players figure he's just going from one stage to another. He's merely 'Sybilizing.'"

One summer a few years later workmen were at our house, adding a new bedroom and putting skylights in the two second-floor bathrooms. One of the carpenters was sitting on the exposed rafters of the open roof, looking down at the field and the practice session below. I knew he was a Bears fan, and I could hear him yell at Ditka—something about how stupid it was to trade away safety Dave Duerson. I heard muffled yelling and then the carpenter came swinging down fast from his perch, looking terrified. What happened?

"Ditka yelled at me," he said, pale as dry wall.

What did he yell?

"'Use your hammer, not your mouth, jackass!'"

While writing this book I took a break to see the soccer comedy movie, *Kicking and Screaming*, starring Will Ferrell and Robert Duvall as kiddie coaches, and Ditka, as—of course—

himself. Enlisted by Ferrell as his assistant, the cigar-chomping Ditka screams on the first day to the assembled 10-year-olds: "I'm not just coaching soccer, *I'M BUILDING MEN!*"

This guy wasn't like Vince Lombardi or Landry or Chuck Noll or Joe Gibbs. Well, maybe there was a bit of Lombardi fury in him. But Ditka was unique. Unlike many high-profile coaches, he had been a great player. He was high strung and ornery, mercurial as a weather vane, and no one had ever considered him a brilliant tactician. But then, his actions were so loud, so unpredictable, nobody much looked at his tactics. He had made so many impetuous mistakes in his life—in judgment, in execution, in choice—that he seemed to be constantly recreating himself out of penance or disgust or boredom into a new, more considerate, more actualized form of human. But through it all he pretty much stayed the same, and he always seemed able to grin at himself.

In his 1992 book, *Monster of the Midway*, Armen Keteyian wrote that Ditka "is some sort of cultural aberration—at once the best and worst his town [Chicago] has produced." It is true Ditka has always carried the positives and the negatives of intense desire with him like twin briefcases, one in each hand. But if he seemed dangerous and threatening long ago, time has softened those ridges. He now is, without argument, Mr. Bear. He has pointedly *stayed* in Chicago after his football career. (Unlike, for instance, Butkus.) Please forget that brief nonsense down there as the New Orleans Saints head coach. (Lord, who else but Ditka would pose for a magazine cover as the groom in a wedding photo with Saints bride/tailback Ricky Williams?)

Ditka has a looming presence that shocks people who stumble into his path. No one could possibly mistake him for anyone but who he is. That head, that brow, those eyes, that walk. Just a few weeks ago a 50-foot wallscape went up at Ohio and LaSalle in Chicago's Loop. The ad is for the Brookfield Zoo, promoting its "Happy Animals, Happy People" campaign, and it shows Ditka's head morphed in a 50-50 tradeoff with a brown bear.

Twenty years have gone by since the Chicago Bears won anything at all, and that was the big one, the Super Bowl. In 1984, my first year in the neighborhood, they showed promise. They beat the evil Los Angeles Raiders for one thing, and they finished a surprising 10-6. They even won a playoff game, the first Bears team to do so in more than two decades.

Then in 1985, not only did they make it to Super Bowl XX, they snatched the champion's mantle and toyed with it and danced on its gilt fabric like maniacs. It was Ditka's pinnacle. It was his fulfilled team. At its crescendo, that 1985 squad was, almost without question, the best NFL team ever. And it was the first to have larger-than-life characters sprinkled throughout. Quasi-nutcases, some. Or maybe it was just the first to have the media appreciate those characters, dissect them, revel in them, despise them, adore them—starting with the head coach. It was a sitcom played out on a runaway train.

I was next door during all of it—except when I was on the road observing the team—stunned like everyone else. To sit down two decades later and have the man himself reflect on the journey has been entertaining, to say the least. Where had he gone, where had the road led?

We did most of the tapings in the cigar bar at Ditka's own restaurant on—where else—Mike Ditka Way, in downtown Chicago. Some we did in the lounge at Bob-o-Link Golf Club in Highland Park, Ditka's home away from home. The tapes are littered with nightclub noises, plates crashing, vacuum cleaners roaring, toasts being proposed, the voices of autograph hounds, singing by empassioned Sinatra devotee John Vincent, wild laughter, shrieking, horrible jokes, pointless digressions, Ditka occasionally bellowing above the din, "Knock it off!" and they are, as you might guess, remarkable.

I couldn't bring Da Coach live to everybody's doorstep. But I captured his thoughts on that classic journey of yore, the one that seems so recent yet recedes daily like a plume of blue cigar smoke over an old oaken bar.

Bon voyage!

—RICK TELANDER
AUGUST 2005

Chapter One

Where Are the Trucks?

The crowd was huge, half a million strong, and the plumes of condensed breath that came from the multitude of cheering mouths dissipated instantly in the stiff breeze. It was January 27, 1986, and downtown Chicago was frozen like a block of dry ice. The temperature was 8 degrees, with a wind chill of 25 below zero. But the adoring masses were out to greet the returning heroes, direct from New Orleans, weather be damned. People barked like rabid dogs. They pounded their mittened hands in joy.

Less than 24 hours earlier the Bears had destroyed the New England Patriots in the Superdome 46-10, the largest margin of victory in any Super Bowl to that date. It wasn't a whipping; it was a humiliation. Consider, for instance, that starting Pats quarterback Tony Eason played all the way into the third quarter yet did not complete a pass.

"If I could crawl out of here," said Patriots linebacker Steve Nelson after the final whistle, "I would."

And the long-starved city of Chicago loved it. Bully for the bullies! On this manic Monday, Mike Ditka rose up through the sun roof of the limousine carrying him in the now-halted victory parade along LaSalle Street. There were hands to shake, supplicants to bless. His army of pilgrims was there, smiling and begging.

I stood up and, believe me, I wasn't hanging out there long. I was in a coat and tie and shades, and it was colder than frozen snot. I'd slept a little the night before, but not a whole lot. There was champagne that had to be drunk, and there was a team party. I did some TV show first thing in New Orleans when I got up—can't remember, *Good Morning America* or *The Today Show* or something—and then we got on the plane and there we were. All those people, and it was really, really cold. It was impressive. It would have been impressive if it had been 80 degrees out, but 25 below? It showed what our team meant to the city of Chicago. To all the Grabowskis.

See, Grabowski is the name I came up with for the players on our team, and it fit Chicago. I grew up in Aliquippa, Pennsylvania, a work-ethic community, where guys went to work with their lunch buckets, did their jobs, and came home with empty lunch buckets. So when we got ready for that second playoff game against the Los Angeles Rams, I said, "We're the Grabowskis, they're the Smiths." I didn't mean anything negative about race or nationality or any of that stuff. It's that we represented Chicago, a work-ethic place. It's just a name I pulled up. A Polish name. It could have been Jim Grabowski, it could have been Tom Grabowski. Hell, it could have been Tinker Bell Grabowski. It symbolized that we were the hard-hat guys. The other guys ride in limos. We ride in trucks.

Of course, there I was in a limo. But like I said, I was freezing my ass off, or at least the part of my body sticking out of the roof. We were all supposed to be in limos, 34 of them, but it was so damn cold that day, even with the sun shining bright, that most of the players were told to stay in the buses. I don't think they minded.

Some of the guys, like Super Bowl MVP Richard Dent, weren't with us. They were already flying to the Pro Bowl in Hawaii. But I knew what Dent had said the night before: "If we're not one of the best teams of all time, I'd like to see the others."

Yeah, that got right to it. We finished 18-1. Fourteen times we held opponents to 10 points or less. We led the league in takeaways, yards given up, all kinds of stuff. Hell, 24 Bears players scored.

Me, I couldn't believe where I was. Mr. Halas had given me a chance. I don't think anybody else would have. There were people right in the Bears organization who didn't want me there, who thought I was the stupidest hire of all time. But Papa

Bear had the say-so—he started the goddamn NFL!—and he gave me the job. I desperately wished he hadn't died two years before, so he could see me, see how I and the team had repaid him for his trust. Because this really was about a team, a group of guys who were kind of misfits who all fit together for that one time.

But, man, the cold! It was crazy.

And there I was, a Grabowski in a limo.

Chapter Two

We'll Be Back!

Mike Singletary stood in back of the team bench at Candlestick Park, facing not the debacle being completed on the field behind him, but the jeering, sneering San Francisco fans.

"Nice game!" hostile voices screamed. A lot of them sounded very drunk. "The Bears suck!"

Singletary's nostrils were flared, and his glinting samurai eyes were wide and focused. He was breathing hard. The clock was running out on this NFC championship game between the Bears and the 49ers, and the Bears were being dissected 23-0. It was January 5, 1985, and Chicago's high hopes for its 1984 team were being crushed. No Super Bowl here. Maybe none ever.

"We'll be back!" Singletary, the Bears' Pro Bowl middle linebacker, yelled in a fevered Southern minister's voice, facing the enemy. "We'll be back! I guarantee you. We WILL be back!"

The crowd hooted and pelted Singletary with more verbal abuse. On the bench Walter Payton had sunken so low into himself it appeared he was shrinking. He may have been crying. He had carried the ball 22 times for 92 yards, and they were hard yards. On one barely successful fourth-and-one run he had to break three tackles—in his own backfield. The Bears' offense was impotent. It had totaled but 186 net yards to the 49ers' 387. And of course, it couldn't score. The loss was complete, overwhelming, destructive. And humiliating. San Francisco coach Bill Walsh had briefly used a 280-pound guard, Guy McIntyre, in his backfield as a flattener. It wasn't illegal. In fact, it was semi-brilliant. But it hurt.

The Bears thought they had a stellar defense, based on the hyper-aggressive "46" scheme. But 49ers quarterback Joe Montana had whipped it by taking three-step drops and throwing in less than two seconds. San Francisco receivers Freddie Solomon and Dwight Clark had 11 catches for 156 yards between them. Bears fill-in quarterback Steve Fuller passed for just 87 yards and was sacked an astounding nine times by a San Francisco defense that was more Bear-ish than the Bears.

Fans began pouring out of the stands before the clock had expired. It was going to get ugly. For the Bears. The refs called the game with two seconds remaining.

Even Singletary, eyes set in fury, ran for the exit.

My God, did we hurt. I don't think anybody can realize how much we hurt after that game. I take the blame for a lot of it, because I thought with our defense, all we'd have to do was stay close, run the ball, and our defense would give us a chance to win. That was wrong. I was wrong. We had to score points, be more aggressive.

I said at the time that we got a lot of lessons out there. In life, you either teach or you learn. Professor or student. I hoped we learned. I was outsmarted by Bill Walsh, their great coach. And I was embarrassed. But we had a couple things going against us, too. Things that had nothing to do with the 49ers.

Our safety Todd Bell had played a great game against the Washington Redskins the week before in our first round, which helped get us into this game—and this NFC title game was as deep into the playoffs as any Bears team had been since the Super Bowl started. But against San Francisco, Bell had to replace our injured right cornerback Les Frazier, and second-year sub Dave Duerson replaced Bell. Later, Bell and Duerson switched positions. Our other safety, Gary Fencik, had a good game with two interceptions. But we were unsettled back there. Neither Todd nor Dave was a cornerback.

Also, we were without Jim McMahon. He was our quarterback, our first-round pick in 1982, my first year. He was smaller than most quarterbacks, and he wasn't in great shape and he was feisty. And he was different. What I was already finding out was that he was going to be injured a lot, because of the way he played. He played balls out, all the time. He had already suffered a lacerated kidney, which in a way was just par

for the course. We'd had four quarterback changes in just that
1984 season because of Jim, but I didn't blame him.

I mean, there was no question that he shortened his career
because of the way he played. He butted heads with linemen, he
ran, he dove, he hung onto the ball too long. He played the way
a linebacker plays the game. He had no regard for his body. But
I couldn't change him. It would have ruined him. His persona
was to put the pedal to the metal, and I kind of liked that. But,
man, the problems.

Fuller couldn't do anything in that NFC game, because we
were playing catch-up most of the time, and they were laying
for him. Steve was a great addition to our team, and tough as
nails himself, but he wasn't McMahon.

Jesus, who was? I remember when McMahon first came to
Chicago. We had just drafted him, and I was in the office with
Jim Finks, the general manager at the time. McMahon walks
into Halas Hall and he's got a beer in his hand and a six-pack
under his arm. I think it was Miller, but it might have been
something else. He has a wad of tobacco under his lip, too. First
thing he says is, "I was getting dry on the way in."

I look at Finks, and he looks at me. Oh, brother. But it was
okay—hell, I played the game, and I did my share of messing
around, and it wasn't going to kill him. He had on a sport coat
and slacks, and sunglasses, of course. He had an eye that was
damaged from when he was a kid—he accidentally stuck a fork
in it or something—and he said he needed the shades for the
pupil. Needed shades all the time. Fine.

After a while it was time for McMahon to talk to Halas. The
Old Man was brutal. He'd only been with the team for 62 years.
When I played, Halas did all the negotiations, all the contracts,
everything. He was tougher than iron. He was mostly retired
now, but he meets McMahon and he looks at him and he says,
"You're not very big, you don't look very strong, your knees are

lousy, you got a bad eye. I'm not going to pay you very much money."

McMahon looks at him, kind of curious. Maybe he yawned. He says, "I thought you drafted me."

Jim was something. Anyway, I knew we weren't bad enough to get shut out, 23-zip by the freaking 49ers. The guys knew it, too. In the locker room afterward I told them I'd take the blame for the mess. I thought we could shove the run at them. I thought we could bully them. I thought we were much more physical than they were. But I realized we would have to be creative and aggressive on offense next time, and we would have to score points.

Were we fighters or not?

And I couldn't forget how Walsh had this formation, and I looked in the backfield, and I'll be damned, there's a guard back there. That big old McIntyre. I said, "Okay. Good. Uh-huh." That stuck in my mind.

I'm talking to the team, and I tell them we will be back and we will play these guys again. I hadn't read it yet, but I know Walsh had a quote in the next day's paper where he said, "They have a great team. When they get their offense squared away with McMahon and get more experience with Fuller and the defensive backfield, I think next year they will be the team to beat."

That's fine. But I was mad as a sledgehammer. I had great respect for Bill. To a point.

I told the team, "We will beat these guys. You take care of the players next time, and I'll take care of the coach."

We had time to think about it. And fume.

Chapter Three

Rope Burns

Platteville, Wisconsin, is not near anything. Unless you consider Tennyson or Belmont or Arthur or Cuba City to be more than dots on a grand agricultural map. But that was the point. The dormant-in-the-summer University of Wisconsin-Platteville made the perfect getaway spot for the Bears' training camp. Away from Chicago—five hours by car, unless you traveled at Payton speed and risked the almost-guaranteed speeding ticket—Platteville offered little but an insulated environment with lots of good flat football fields and meeting rooms and dorms far from prying eyes. Well, that wasn't entirely true. Members of the Chicago sports media would reluctantly make the trip—bitching the whole way—and fans from southern Wisconsin and northwestern Illinois and eastern Iowa would pile into the family cars to make the hot summer trips to watch the Bears go through preseason camp.

But Platteville was a place for the Bears to come together and focus on the season ahead with relatively few distractions. In July 1985, that focus was keen and narrow. The coach was fired up. So were the veterans. Still, it wasn't as pleasant and unified an atmosphere as it could have been.

Two key defensive members of the Bears' 1984 team were holding out, looking for better contracts. Safety Todd Bell and linebacker/defensive end Al Harris did not report to Platteville with their mates. Singletary had been disgruntled with his salary, too, and was, at least in theory, a brief holdout. But the Bears restructured his contract, and he showed up on time. Harris and Bell, however, would not show up all year. It became one of the sad parts of the 1985 Bears' journey, a journey with so many epic overtones that would lead others to unique places—that two respected members of the stepping-stone unit would not be along for the ride.

And yet the band traveled onward, without the pair. Both Bell and Harris suffered from their exclusion, from the knowledge that

*business matters sometimes can't trump personal loss. Of the two,
Bell took it the hardest.*

*There was tragic irony when, in mid-March 2005, Bell
suffered a heart attack while driving his car in suburban
Columbus, Ohio, crashing into a house. His death came the day
after the Bears' Super Bowl players and coaches publicly agreed to
work together with Bears management, often their enemy, on
celebrating and capitalizing on the impending 20th-year
anniversary of Super Bowl XX. The agreement was festively
promoted in the Chicago media, with the* Sun-Times *even
running a color photo of alumni Otis Wilson, Dennis McKinnon,
Steve McMichael, Dent, and Fencik grinning wide in front of a
Super Bowl XX logo, festooned with the group's website:
www.85worldchamps.com. Once again Bell had been reminded of
what he had lost. Fellow holdout Harris told the* Chicago Tribune,
*"Todd never let 1985 go. He felt betrayed. I had that feeling, too,
but after a while, that's life."*

Todd Bell was 47.

I liked Todd a lot. But I never understood his holdout. Al's,
either. Todd had Howard Slusher as his agent, and that was
Slusher's technique—sit out until you get what you want. Or
don't play. I know players don't have much clout, but that was
the biggest mistake of their careers.

Todd wanted something like a $1.5 million for three years,
and Jerry Vainisi, our GM, was offering a million. Al wanted, I
don't know, maybe a hundred grand more a year than was
offered. Todd was a hitter. He was a banger. In the Washington
playoff game the season before he changed the tempo of the
game. We only won 23-19, and he put a lick on their running
back, Joe Washington, that was unbelievable.

Al was in between a linebacker and a defensive end; he was
a slipper and a slider. You could put him up or you could put

him down. Maybe he wasn't the fastest guy, but he was agile enough and he had a great wingspan. He used his weight well. And he was one of the nicest guys I'd ever been around, which just made it all so hard. But we had Duerson to replace Bell, and Wilbur Marshall had just finished his rookie year, and I knew he was going to be a star and could play where Harris was. If we moved Dan Hampton to defensive end from tackle and moved this huge new kid, William Perry, in next to Steve McMichael and did some other things, we would be set to go.

Actually, when you got down to it, Todd was limited. He was a blitzer, a guy who could tackle really hard, but he had no coverage ability. He was almost like a linebacker. That was part of the deal with the "46" defense—it was named after old safety Doug Plank, No. 46, and Plank was just a big hitter, like Todd. I went in before camp to talk to Jerry Vainisi, and he said, "Mike, we're not gonna get these deals done with these two guys."

That was hard to take, but I thought about it, and I said, "We'll play without them." That might sound cocky on my part, but I thought we could replace them. And I wanted to reward the guys who were in camp and had been busting their asses. They'd done everything we asked, and I wasn't going to spit on them. You're with us or you're not.

I knew how the Bears were with money, how they'd always been. I came in as a rookie first-round pick in 1961 and got $12,000 and a $6,000 bonus. Then I went on to catch 56 passes for over 1,000 yards and 12 touchdowns and was named Rookie of the Year and made the Pro Bowl. The next year Halas tried to pay me *less*. You had to talk to the Old Man himself, face to face, in those deals. It was like looking at Mt. Rushmore. I finally got him all the way back up to $18,000, what I'd made the year before. Man. But playing the game was the main thing; it always was.

Buddy Ryan was our defensive coordinator, and when I told him he wouldn't have Bell and Harris, he almost went nuts. Buddy was a holdover from when Neill Armstrong was head coach, as were most of the assistants. I know he thought Halas should have named him the next head coach, but there was nothing I could do about that. That didn't help the tension between us.

At any rate, I talked to Todd and Al through the years, and it was always a little sad. They both came back the next year, but it wasn't the same. They weren't starters, and they weren't going to be. That summer at the start of camp, though, I told our guys I believed in loyalty and I'd reward it. We were going to the Super Bowl because we had the players we needed.

Otis Wilson was there when I arrived in 1982, and so were Fencik and Walter and a lot of guys. We drafted Mike Richardson and Marshall and Reggie Phillips and Jim Covert, whom I thought was the best pick I ever made, at left tackle. We had Keith Van Horne and Jay Hilgenberg and Mark Bortz and Tom Thayer on the O-line, and McKinnon and Gault at receivers and Tim Wrightman and Emery Moorehead, who gave me so much, at tight end, and we had Maury Buford as our new punter and Kevin Butler as the kicker.

We had Mike Singletary in the middle on defense, a guy they'd tell you now was too small to play or some damn thing. Right. Because they don't measure your fricking heart! And, of course, we had Walter Payton in the middle on offense. He is to this day the greatest football player I've ever seen. Not the biggest. Not the fastest. Not the anything. Just the best player who ever played.

We had all kinds of people on that club, but they were focused like I was. Covert, I mean, on the first day he came to the Bears in 1983 I just said, "There's left tackle, That's yours."

And he never let me down. He had a short career because he hurt his back, but what a warrior he was.

We had been building this team, and a lot of pieces were there before I came. The Bears were long known as a defensive team. But you had to have a quarterback, a good one. Otherwise we were never going to win. I remember all of the conversations Coach Halas and Jim Finks had about Vince Evans, who came in 1977, about what a great, great athlete he was. Yeah, he was a great athlete, but he wasn't a winner. Good or bad, that's just the way it was.

See, I played with a winner in Dallas, a guy named Staubach. I knew what it took to play the position and be great—hell, Roger Staubach's in the Hall of Fame. Maybe it took a cocky guy. Maybe not. You could have a calm guy like Roger, a guy who led by example, a guy who was smart, who you'd want in the foxhole with you. He was a military guy, remember. He never berated you, but he knew how to get you to do what was needed. It was plain old leadership, but deep inside it was cockiness—he knew that he could lead.

Now, we took McMahon with the first pick when I had just gotten to the Bears, and he had a different kind of brashness. The one problem he had was with authority. He had a problem with his father, he had a problem with his Brigham Young coach, and he had a problem with me. Authority figures. He was defiant just because he didn't want to be known as a conformist, or a guy who would listen. He sure as hell didn't care about being an All-American boy.

But his teammates, especially the offense, believed in him. I guess I had a problem a little like his. In 1982 Ed McCaskey, the chairman of the board, who was married to Virginia Halas, the Old Man's daughter, called me in. Ed and Virginia had a lot of kids, and their oldest son, Michael, was soon going to be president and CEO of the Bears. But Ed and Jim Finks wanted

Michael McCaskey smiled a lot in 1985. Wonder why. *Jonathan Daniel/Getty Images*

to talk to me about something or other I'd said in the paper. I came in and they both went at me, telling me I couldn't say whatever it was that I said. I honestly don't remember. And they're both dead.

But I do remember I told them, "Here's what I'm going to do. I'm going to leave here and go to my office and call Mr. Halas, and I'm going to ask who's running this football team." So I got him on the line and I said, "Mr. Halas, I have to know—who do I answer to, you or them?"

He said, "Kid, you only answer to me."

Maybe that wasn't an authority problem I had, but it was a control issue. And the thing is, Halas had been tough with me and he gave me crap after my very first game as head coach. It was at Detroit, and we lost 17-10. We had two different chances to score from the one-yard line and we didn't make it. The next morning I came into my office and there is the play book opened to the page that says, "Quarterback Sneak." Jesus, was he pissed off!

Anyway, here we are in camp and we have to rally together, all of us. The ones who are here. The ones ready for this goal. McMahon may have been a jerk—I remember his first year he ran the mile and a half in almost 13 minutes, walking the last part, looking like he was going to puke and die, behind everybody but our very heavy offensive lineman Noah Jackson—but he was on board. I read that in 1984, even with his lacerated kidney, he'd gone out for Halloween with his teammates, dressed as a priest, drunk. He had a Bible with him, and I guess when you opened it, there were photos of naked women inside. Well, this was football, not religion.

There in Platteville we came together, because there wasn't anyplace to go. We had a pig roast or something and the corn fields were all around. Some of the guys rode scooters everywhere, and I guess that was a little risky. One year Van

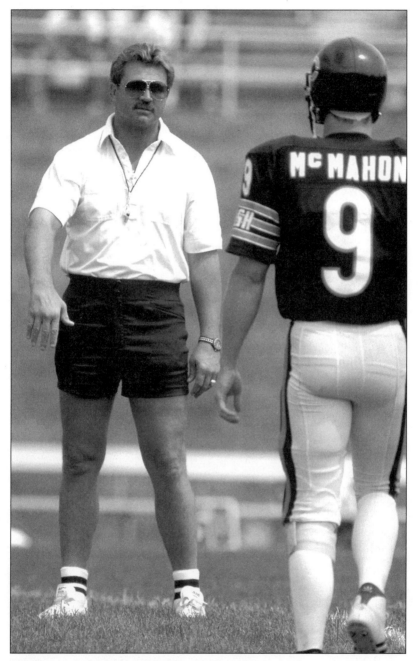

The shorts may have been high and tight, but the team was loose, and McMahon was looser. *Jonathan Daniel/Getty Images*

Horne, a huge guy at six foot eight, ran into a rope across a sidewalk or something, and if he hadn't been so tall he might have been decapitated. As it was, he just got some nice rope burns on his biceps.

We knew we were a pretty good team in 1984. And in 1985 we knew we were better, even if we had issues. Screw the issues.

We were ready to kick ass.

Chapter Four

No Saints Here

As the 1985 season approached, the Bears were evolving into a team with as much personality as football talent. It was a good thing Platteville was far away from major civilization, because there was a sense that Ditka's odd crew might not have withstood close scrutiny from discreet society or perhaps even the law.

Second Street was the name of the Platteville lane with the bars frequented by the Bears after hours. Players could do almost anything, according to Ditka rule, as long as they didn't get arrested or hurt. Pranks and acting crazy were fine, as long as nobody blew out a knee, ripped a hammy, broke a bone. There is a photo taken during spring practice before they left for Platteville, and it shows the dynamic backfield tandem of fullback Matt Suhey and tailback Walter Payton getting set before a play. The interesting part is that Payton has the startled Suhey's gym shorts waistband in his hand, pulling it down low and back like a slingshot. Ditka didn't care. All he wanted was to win.

Platteville is Platteville, you know what I mean? The first couple years we'd played in Lake Forest, and there were too many kids and mothers and all that around. Hangers-on everywhere. I thought we could bond better up in the boondocks. I know the guys went out at night. They had fun, and that was okay. They weren't a bunch of saints. John Madden used to have a coaching philosophy that went: be on time, pay attention, and play like hell. And that pretty much sums it up. I know Van Horne almost killed himself on that scooter, but when I was playing, I remember we were running across a field trying to get away from the cops who were chasing us, and a couple of the guys tripped over wires strung between two posts and almost broke their legs in half. That's football. There's a time to play and a time to have fun. If it's all drudgery, I don't think you can win. I mean, these guys aren't fruits. They are who they are. Even a stoic guy like Tom Landry, my coach when

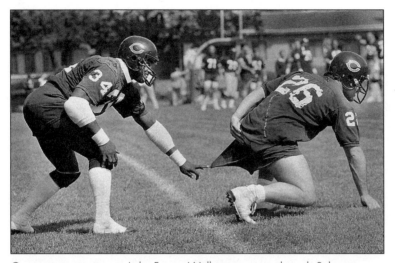

Our spring minicamp in Lake Forest. Wally prepares to launch Suhey on to Platteville, where the real work will begin. *Photo by Jim Maentanis*

I was in Dallas, let guys have fun. Actually, he didn't know what guys were doing. He could have known, but he didn't want to know. That's a choice. That was "America's Team" with this clean-cut image. But the things guys were doing were off the charts. Still, we showed up every day, practiced our asses off, and played like hell on Sundays. That's what I wanted from my guys.

Looking back at all these clippings from 1985, I can see that we were like a three-ring circus. There was something going on every day. I didn't read the papers back then, so I had no idea how nuts things were. But I know I tried to deflect some of the attention onto me, because I didn't want the players under any pressure except to go out and play. If the press thought I was an asshole, fine. Didn't bother me. I was on a mission from the moment I took the job.

And the success could have happened sooner. I blew the first game I coached in 1982, up there in Detroit, by not scoring from the one-yard line, twice! It made me feel bad, but it made Mr. Halas feel a hell of a lot worse. And I wanted to please him. I wanted him to know I was worthy, and a Bear through and through.

My first week as coach I gathered everybody together and said, "This is going to be a good news-bad news announcement. The good news is we are going to win the Super Bowl. The bad news is a lot of you who don't care enough aren't going to be with us when it happens." I meant that. We had a lot of selfish guys back in 1982, but I knew the Fenciks and Paytons and Suheys and Hamptons would be with me.

See, George Halas embodied the Bears, and I wanted to embody them, too. Not many people know this, but in 1978 I wrote Mr. Halas a letter. I was the special teams coach for the Cowboys, and I was no big deal. Maybe I was a little wild. But what I said in the letter was, "We didn't part on the best of terms when you traded me, but I would love to come back some day, back to Chicago. And be the head coach. I'm not ready yet, but I will be some day. I'll bring back Chicago Bears tradition and pride. I promise."

Sid Luckman, the great old Bears quarterback, told me Halas always kept that letter. Sid and Mr. Halas were best friends. See, for me, it was the Bears only. I wanted nothing else. It was my ultimate goal. Just the Bears. That and winning the Super Bowl.

A few years went by, and then after the Cowboys lost to the 49ers in the 1981 playoffs, a really tough game where Dwight Clark made that great catch from Montana in the end zone, Coach Landry called me into his office.

"There's somebody who wants to talk to you," he said.

"Who?" I asked.

"George Halas of the Bears."

It excited the hell out of me. Tom gave me his blessing, and I got on a plane to Chicago. It was all cloak and dagger there, with Halas's right-hand man Max Swiatek, his driver and longtime helper, picking me up at the airport and taking me to Halas's place at the Edgewater Beach condos up on the north side near Lake Michigan. We sat at the kitchen table and he asked me some stuff. I was really keyed up, and I knew it wasn't him when he said, "What's your philosophy about football?"

"Coach, who are you kidding?" I said. "My philosophy is exactly the same as yours. My philosophy is to make the Bears something special, and to kick people's asses!"

He just nodded. He looked right at me. He said, "Okay, I'm going to give you a three-year contract to be our new head coach. One hundred thousand dollars a year. That's it."

I said, "No."

He was stunned. "What do you mean? You can't do it?"

"No," I said. "I will do it. But I have to have a 15 percent raise each year."

I thought I was really being a cool ass. Hell, that would still make me one of the lowest-paid coaches in the league. But it didn't matter. It wasn't about money. Nobody else had offered me anything. It was just something to show I was my own man.

So he gave me the deal—$100,000, $115,000, $130,000— and we shook hands, signed the contract, and that was that. But what I really wanted was his respect. I meant it when I wrote that letter. I felt the Bears were my destiny. And George Halas *was* the Bears. His son Mugs Halas had died, and that left George's only other child, Virginia, and all her children as heirs to the family business.

But I knew deep inside he believed in me, the outsider, the old tight end. I think he believed that I was a lot like him. When he was lying in the hospital a year or so later, there were only two people he wanted to see—his secretary, Ruth, and me. Nobody else. I talked to him about the players we had just drafted. I told him he'd like Covert, that he was kind of similar to old-time star Joe Stydahar, and the Old Man liked that. He was very sick at that time, but he told Ruth to give me a special bottle of champagne he had. "Give this to Mike," he told her. "For when they win the Super Bowl."

It makes me sad because the bottle is out there on the wall, in a place of honor in my restaurant, and he wasn't alive when we opened it.

But I didn't know what was going to happen. I told the players they deserved to win it all, but nobody could foresee the future.

We came out for the opening game against the Tampa Bay Buccaneers and we felt we were in a good position. Platteville had been hot and tough, and Buddy had his defensive unit in good shape from all of the running they did. My guys, the offense, were ready to go, too, especially since McMahon was back for his first start since the kidney injury the previous November. I figured beer must have been part of his cure. Maybe it filtered out the bad stuff.

We were favored by a touchdown or so, partly because the Bucs were playing in Chicago, partly because our defense was so good, and partly because their star defender, Lee Roy Selmon, was out. We'd set the NFL sack record the year before, so everybody was sure our defense would dominate.

But it didn't. We gave up 28 points in the first two quarters, over 300 yards in the game, and were down 21-7 early and then 28-17 at the half. It was September 8, and it was hotter than blazes on our artificial turf at Soldier Field, something like 137 degrees at turf level. Maybe that's why the fans booed us when we came off at the half, because they were roasting. But I don't

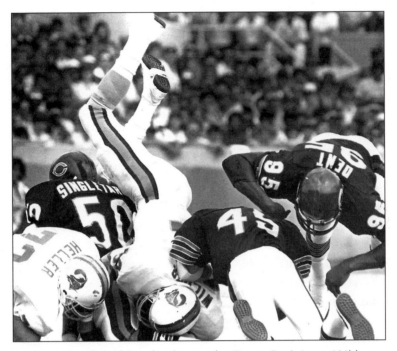

Singletary, Fencik, and Dent lay the wood to Tampa Bay's James Wilder.
Jonathan Daniel/Getty Images

think so. We weren't playing as a unit. This offensive and defensive split wasn't good. We had to be one.

Fortunately, McMahon was on target, and Payton was running the way he could. Walter carried the ball 17 times for 120 yards, and Jim completed 23 of 34 passes for 274 yards and two TDs. He also ran for two scores, and didn't hurt his kidney in the process, for which I was thankful. It was nice the offense bailed out our defense for once. In fact, that helped us all, because, like I said, there was some tension between the two sides. And it was nice that McMahon got NFC Player of the Week honors for leading the charge. But it wasn't a game to be thrilled about. I was proud that our offense proved it could strike back. But we all knew we needed that D if we were going to go anywhere.

If we had lost that game, people would have said, "I told you so! You bums were nothing but a flash in the pan! San Francisco sucked you dry!'"

I thought back to the previous three years I'd been coaching the Bears. At the beginning we were losing all of these games we should have won. It worried me. But then we had Bob Avellini playing quarterback, and he was one of the biggest screw-ups I'd ever met. I had no idea what he'd do.

We're playing out in Seattle in 1984, and Avellini is starting because McMahon—guess what?—is already out with an injury. We're ahead, 7-0, Payton's averaging over five yards a carry, and it's second and four, and we have a nice play called. Oh yeah, we're undefeated at the time—3-0. Then I hear Ed Hughes, our offensive coordinator, standing next to me, say, "Oh, no."

"What, Ed?" I yell.

"The son of a bitch is audible-ing!"

Avellini audibles to a hitch, from a fly pattern with max protection, and the Seattle cornerback picks the ball off on a dead run and he's going so fast in the other direction for a touchdown he nearly breaks his neck when he hits the end zone wall. Bob comes out of the game, which we went on to lose, 38-9, and I say—shit, I am trembling—"Bob, why would you do that, son?"

"Well, I thought—"

"Don't THINK!" I scream. "Please. Don't." Then I add, "Bob, if you ever do that again you will never—ever—EVER—play another down for me! *DO YOU UNDERSTAND ME?*"

He nods.

Then we're up in Green Bay the next year, and he does the same exact damn thing. I was purple. I was green. I was sub-human.

"That's it!" I screamed. "You're done!"

He looks at me and says, "Well, you never liked me anyway."

"Don't LIKE you?! You #%&*!@+!!%—!—"

I was going to kill him. Right there. Tear his flesh off like a jackal. I was so mad my neck veins had veins. Everybody was holding me back. I mean: *He did the same thing!*

Years later we were playing the Vikings up at that indoor roller rink they have in Minneapolis, and Jim Harbaugh was my quarterback. I said before the game, "It's gonna be loud out there. No audibles. Your linemen can't hear. I'm not going to put you in position to call a play that won't work. Okay? Got it?" Harbaugh nodded. Everybody nodded.

In the game we're beating the Vikings, 20-0, and I have a fly route to Gault called. Up the sideline. Harbaugh audibles to a hitch. Interception! We lose the game 21-20. There are photos that ran after that where I'm getting ready to strangle Harbaugh. I was wrong on the sideline, and I've calmed down through the years, and two wrongs don't make a right. BUT I DON'T UNDERSTAND WHEN PEOPLE DO THINGS LIKE THAT! Call the goddamn play!

Now the thing about McMahon was he was out there on his own, too, and he'd drive you crazy with audibles. But he could read a defense, he was a master at seeing the field, and he could sense the blitz.

So we had a chance with Jimmy Mac. Thing was, would the little turd survive? In 1984 he missed seven games plus the playoffs with everything from a hairline fracture of his hand to a bad back to that kidney thing.

In 1984 when we played the Raiders, was about the most brutal game I'd ever seen. I told my players we had to beat them, it was the only way to get to the next level, to prove to ourselves we belonged. The Raiders knocked out Jim, could have killed him with that kidney injury. And we knocked out their quarterback. Guys were getting carried off the field left and right. I think the Raiders even had to put Ray Guy, their punter, in at quarterback. But we won 17-6 over the mighty Raiders. Our defense kicked ass. Our record was 7-3, but McMahon was done for the year, and we couldn't sustain. You gotta have a quarterback. I realized that.

McMahon was back now, and I prayed he would last. I know I was frothing at the mouth half of the time early in my career. He annoyed me so much—I swear he would wear stupid clothes or say crazy things on the sideline or to the press or grab the mike and blabber on the team plane or go out and get plastered, just to make me boil.

But I knew this. If you're going to be the bully, you have to beat the bully. And the bullies were everywhere.

And we needed this crazy quarterback. We were 1-0, just getting started.

Chapter Five

Bodyslams and All-Day Suckers

The New England Patriots were coming to town. Coached by Raymond Berry, the Patriots had won their first game and had a fierce defense and a workable offense directed by third-year quarterback Tony Eason. Nobody knew that New England might figure into the Bears' journey somewhere else along the trail. For now all that mattered was keeping the dream alive, the quest.

One issue that popped up again during the week was the sometimes harmless, but sometimes nasty rivalry between the Bears' offense and defense. A fight had broken out in practice midweek between offensive guard Mark Bortz and defensive tackle Steve McMichael, Actually, there had been two fights between the men. Fights can show intensity and desire. But they can also show pettiness and lack of respect. Ditka was a little worried about this last mini-brawl.

I guarantee you I never moved three feet when the fight happened between Bortz and McMichael, and I don't think Buddy moved, either. It wasn't that I wasn't concerned, but some things have to be settled without a lot of interference. And what could I do, anyway?

McMichael, that's just the way he was. He was a tough Texas boy, a free agent we picked up because he had tons of heart. He was a little out there at times. They said he wore his clothes in camp until he had a pile of dirty stuff, then he just turned the pile over and wore it all again. One of his hobbies was rattlesnake hunting. But he would get in your face and never shy away from anything. I love Steve McMichael. Bortz was quiet, a six-foot-six, 270-pound guy from a little town in Wisconsin, who had been a defensive player and co-captain at Iowa. He was a defensive lineman before he switched to offense in the NFL, so maybe that had the two of them going a little bit.

Steve McMichael was rough and tough, but like everybody else, he had to learn to respect our offense. *Photo by Vernon J. Biever*

One problem we had was we were always going against our own defense in practice, and sometimes they were so fired up that we couldn't get a damn thing accomplished. I'd yell at Buddy, "For Chrissake, we're not playing the Bears next week!" But there was tension—football is a mean game—and those defensive players had great chemistry and great pride. Buddy had them cranked up like assassins. They'd run that "46," and it was like there were 50 killers on the line ready to slit your throat.

But then—and I think it may have been a week or so after we had bailed out the defense against Tampa Bay—we finally got the defense's respect. The exact date of a lot of these things gets blurry. It wasn't like I was keeping a diary, and after coaching the Bears for 11 years, I may get some things jumbled. But you don't forget the moments that jump out at you, the ones that changed things. At any rate, we were at practice, no media was around, and McMichael was mouthing off to the offensive line. Who knows who he was pissed at. But Jim Covert just grabbed him and body-slammed him. Now I love Steve, as I've said. He never complained about anything, fought through any pain he had. And he was a tough guy. But Covert was a high school wrestler in Pennsylvania who had pinned all but one of his opponents his senior year. He was quick and agile. He was one of the quietest guys on the team. He'd been an English major in college. He'd gone to Pitt, my old school, and he was best friends with Danny Marino. But he could be pushed only so far, and you did not want to mess with him.

He slammed McMichael, who would go on to be a pro wrestler—one of those guys hitting other guys over the head with folding chairs and briefcases—and it showed the defense we weren't taking any more shit off them. It ended as quickly as it began. There was silence for a bit, and then I blew the whistle

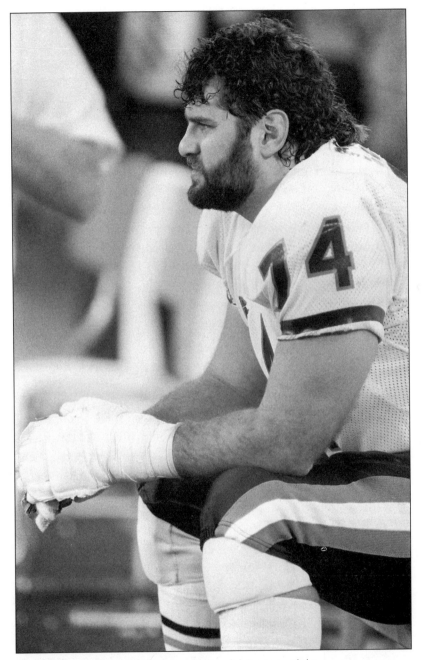

Jim Covert was quiet and low key, but you didn't mess with him.
Jonathan Daniel/Getty Images

and said, "Let's get back to practice." You'd be surprised how much that ended the crap.

I coached the offense. Buddy had the defense. That's just the way it was. But a team doesn't have two sides, it has one. And the respect has to go back and forth, between everybody. McMichael made our guys better by the way he practiced. Nobody liked it at times. It wasn't a picnic out there. It was not a walk in the park. We were in pads every day up until Saturday.

The point is we had an offense that controlled the ball for a reason. We knew that if we gave our defense enough time to rest, they could go out and be animals. Who gives a damn if you won 40 to 30, or 10 to nothing? Actually, I like 10 to nothing. So our offense led the league in first downs and time of possession by design. We needed respect. Just as our defense already had respect.

Buddy was tough on his guys. He ran them, had them do ladder drills, ups-and-downs, and there were times when I'd have to tell him to stop. My offense was conditioned, too, but like with the receivers, they ran their asses off all practice long, so what was the point of running them at the end? But Buddy believed in those whistle drills for his guys. They hated them, but they never, ever quit, because they knew the reason for doing them. The defensive guys were as tough at the end of games as they were on the opening series. They were *in shape*. Buddy had their total attention and total respect.

As a coach, it was never about me. I had a bad temper and I got crazed at times, but what I wanted was to win. And when a team wins, everybody wins. It's about challenging the other team, doing everything you can with every bone in your body, because losing is rotten. When I got traded from the Eagles to the Cowboys, I went from being a pretty good individual player to being a team player, because I realized my value was not in catching 60 passes a year—they had guys to do that. What they needed from me was to angle block, pass block, take out linebackers for the runners behind me like Calvin Hill or Duane Thomas or Walt Garrison or Dan Reeves, whoever was carrying the ball. I understood how important I was to the team, not how important I was to myself. That Super Bowl championship ring the Cowboys won in 1971, when we beat Miami 24-3, sure felt good on my finger.

I suppose, right from the get go, teamwork and foresight by other people were part of my pro career. In college I'd played both ways, and the teams that wanted me—Washington, Pittsburgh, and San Francisco—were going to make me play linebacker. But the Bears took me, and the Old Man said, "You're a tight end." Did anyone know what a tight end was back then? Not really.

The whole idea of a big guy in close catching a lot of passes was kind of new. We played the Eagles in 1961, and a linebacker named Chuck Weber grabbed me and threw me down. He lined up right over me and forced me outside, and I couldn't do anything, and then he'd force me in, and the middle linebacker would knock me on my ass. Sometimes both of them would pound me, hold me down. I told Halas, "Those guys are holding me, Coach! Pushing me in, out—I can't do anything."

He and Luke Johnsos—the wide receivers coach, but really the offensive coordinator, even though we didn't have those titles back then—discussed this, and then Halas said to me, "Flex out two to five yards. Put the outside guy on an island. See what he does with that."

So I flex out on some of the pass plays and some of the runs, almost like a slot. What happens when I run a slant now? If I'm blocking the linebacker on a run, he's already out of the play. He's not gonna be a factor. We did it, and it worked. I mean why run through someone when you can run around them? Well, okay, sometimes you just gotta knock the crap out of a

McMahon and Payton celebrate in the first New England game, maybe the hardest hit Walter took. *Jonathan Daniel/Getty Images*

guy, because it is football, and kicking ass is fun. But how many great players are you going to intimidate?

You think you could intimidate Chuck Bednarik? Hah! Break his arm off and he'd throw it at you. How are you going to intimidate Ronnie Lott? Or Dan Hampton? Or Mike Singletary or Walter Payton? You might beat them, but you're not going to intimidate them, not because they're scared of what you're doing. Hell, no. Yeah, you beat the yolk out of people. But you outsmart them, too.

I had run-ins with guys like the Packers' Ray Nitschke, that bald guy who tried to tear my head off constantly. I had run-ins with a lot of great players. I hit them high, I hit them low—and they hit me that way, too. Bill Pellington, the Colts' linebacker, was wearing my ass out one game. He was slugging me, and I was slugging him. And finally I ended up with this cloth thing on my arm with a hunk of lead at the end, like a freaking weapon. I ran to the official and said, "That asshole's trying to kill me with a chunk of lead!"

The ref grabbed it out of my hand and said, "Gimme that, you idiot. It's my flag!" He threw it at us and it hit my arm. I was so embarrassed.

Pellington looked at me and said, "Ditka, I don't need lead to beat your sorry ass!"

Anyway, the Patriots game—game two of the regular season—begins and our defense is back to what it should be, an attacking force. The offense had come from behind in the Tampa Bay game to win that one, and now the defense is returning the favor.

They're going after Eason and the Patriots runners like they're free beer. It was kind of funny, because on Friday I happened to see this stupid-ass thing called the Dunkel Rating in a newspaper that was lying open. I also saw that our defense was ranked 23rd against the rush, even though it had led the league in rushing defense the year before. One game. Fricking statistics! And this Dunkel thing had the Bears rated only 12th best out of the 28 NFL teams. Fine. Screw 'em all. Dumb-ass Rating is more like it. We'll see how it ends.

McMahon started off the game with a 32-yard touchdown pass to Dennis McKinnon, who was still battling back from off-season knee surgery. Dennis was a skinny guy, but like the guys I loved on this team, just tough and nasty, and he'd give you everything he had. That 7-0 lead was all we needed. New

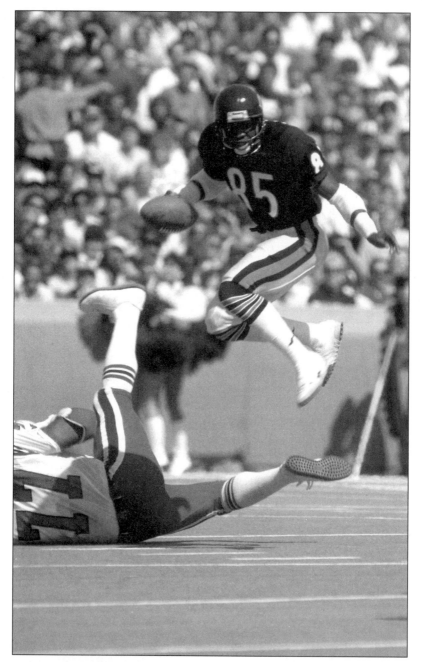

Dennis McKinnon was an intense, mouthy, skinny guy who did nothing but make big plays. *Jonathan Daniel/Getty Images*

England couldn't do a thing against our defense. They had 27 yards rushing, and Eason got sacked half a dozen times and threw three interceptions. They wouldn't have scored at all except for a mistake on coverage when fullback Craig James caught a little pass across the middle and outran Wilbur Marshall for a 90-yard score in the fourth quarter. We were up 20-0 before that, and we won 20-7. Take away that pass and they only had 116 net yards. We had 369.

What I liked was the Patriots had six sacks the week before, and they got none against us. Our offensive line of Tom Thayer, Jay Hilgenberg, Keith Van Horne, Jimbo Covert, and Mark Bortz was developing into a cohesive unit. It's so important to have that communication and camaraderie when blocking, the same guys lining up together day after day, knowing each other's traits and techniques and personalities. We had that working now.

The Patriots keyed all game long on Payton, who was a little beaten up going in, and he only gained 39 yards. No problem. That opened up other things, including 37 yards rushing for backup Thomas Sanders and a TD run for Suhey. We also got two field goals from our rookie kicker Kevin Butler, a fourth-round draft pick out of Georgia. Butthead's addition had meant I had to let vet Bob Thomas go at the end of the preseason. Butler went on to set an NFL rookie scoring record in 1985, so Bob knew what he was up against. But I loved Bob Thomas. He was a great guy. Butler wasn't any more accurate, but he kicked off much deeper, so there was nothing I could do.

Oh, I didn't like cutting Bob. I never liked that part. I sat down with him, and it was miserable. It's the hardest thing you do as a coach. When I released defensive lineman Mike Hartenstine after 1986, it broke my heart. But there's a time when it has to happen, and you're the only one who can do it. Nobody teaches you how. I watched Coach Landry do it, and I watched him break down. I'd hear him tell a coach, "I'm keeping this man because he's a better football player, but I'm cutting a man who has so much more character." Oh, it hurt him!

I believe in loyalty. I thought about all that because we were playing without Bell and Harris, and people were saying the defense really missed them. It actually was tragic that they weren't with us, in a way. But you can't move on unless better players replace lesser ones, and the guys you have replace the guys you don't have. Loyalty only goes so far. Character only goes so far. Football is played with talent and speed and mean.

And I think Bob Thomas did okay, too, probably better than any of us. He went back to school, got his law degree, and now he's the chief justice of the Illinois Supreme Court.

Make no mistake about it—we *were* a talented team. Hell, we had 10 first-round draft picks on the club—a lot of them from Jim Finks, and some from Jerry Vainisi and me. In the entire league, only the Packers had more first-round guys with 11.

One of our first-round guys, Mike Singletary, had a hell of a game, too. He had three sacks and an interception. What a competitor he was. What a student of the game. Another first-rounder, William Perry, our rookie 315-pound or 300-whatever-pound defensive tackle from Clemson, didn't get in much. But before the game the Patriots' center, Pete Brock, was asked about him. "That's an all-day sucker!" he said. But Buddy wasn't using Perry much. Big Bill already had his nickname, "The Refrigerator," and I felt we ought to plug that appliance in somewhere. Things were going through my mind. I was daydreaming and thinking and calculating.

Mostly, I was happy we got out of this one pretty easily. McMahon's back was a little stiff, so we rested him at the end and put in Fuller.

But there was no time to sit around and feel good about being 2-0. The NFL schedule was all about entertainment and not about sanity or what was good for us.

We had the asshole Vikings in four days.

Chapter Six

A Dog on My Ankle

As we wrote this book, Ditka and I referred frequently to the loose-leaf 500-page binder that contained photocopied pages of Chicago newspaper sports reports from late 1984 all the way into early 1986. Sometimes Ditka would drift off, becoming so intent in his reading that his wife, Diana, and I would sit at the table in the restaurant, facing him, and talk about him almost as if he were not in the room. One time Mike borrowed his wife's reading glasses to see some especially fine print, and Diana cracked up watching this huge, oblivious man with the big, ruddy, circular, mustachioed face, studying newsprint while wearing tiny, rhinestone-encrusted glasses.

Invariably Ditka would look up from his reading and say something about the craziness of that 1985 season, marveling at the whirlwind of gossip and excitement and anticipation and drama that surrounded the team and himself, and how he was basically unaware of that sideshow element to the quest.

"I almost never read the papers," he said. "I never realized what was going on unless somebody told me. I guess we were a little different, huh?"

He did have a weekly TV show on CBS during the season— hosted by former Bears teammate Johnny Morris—that became something of a local legend, with fans going crazy during the tapings and nobody ever quite sure how any episode would end.

At 2-0 the frenzy knob was slowly being turned up for Ditka's boys, especially because there would be a third game in the first 17 days of the season—on a non-Thanksgiving Thursday, for goodness sake—and the Bears were playing their third undefeated team in a row. (Yes, technically, Tampa Bay was unbeaten in the season opener.) Moreover, the Minnesota Vikings were a perennial spear in the side of the Bears, much like the Packers were. The Vikings had dignified history on their side with their icily stoic icon of a coach, Bud Grant, at the helm once again, after a year off. And the Vikes had been to four Super Bowls in the 19 years since the "ultimate game" began. The Bears, of course, had been to none.

Playing on a Thursday night, with one day being needed mostly for travel, was a tough pill for the Bears to swallow. But it was nothing compared to the swift excitement after the Patriots game. For Ditka this was becoming a short week from hell. And the national media was starting to pay full attention to every tiny thing that came from the Bears camp, every word, every gesture, every bit of nonsense.

I didn't get crazy excited after the New England win, but I guess I shouldn't even have smiled. I thought McMahon had made it through in good shape. But there he was on Monday at Lake Forest Hospital, in traction.

I couldn't believe it.

I don't know when he hurt his back. And he didn't know for sure, either. It could have been from as far back as the Tuesday before the game. It could have been on the first play of the game. It could have been while opening beer cans. But there he was, again, hurt. The year before he missed seven regular-season games, plus the playoffs because of injuries. This uncertainty, I knew by now, would probably be a theme for Jim's whole career. It would probably make me check into a mental facility.

By Tuesday he was wearing a big immobilizing collar around his neck, but he couldn't practice, and I knew I was going to have to use Fuller, with Mike Tomczak as the backup quarterback. I mean, if you don't practice, how in the hell can you play? But right away Jim started yapping about how there was "no possibility" he wouldn't play. There were camera crews around. Joe Namath, Jim's old childhood hero, I guess, had come to town to do something for TV about Mac. This was a big national game we were playing, and I knew everybody was fired up. But I'd let McMahon play four games in 1984 with a broken hand, and we'd lost two and been trailing when he came out of another. If he was hurt now, he was out. This was my new rule. Jesus, the guy was too sore even for his chiropractor to work on him!

Other guys were banged up a little, too. Walter had bad ribs, maybe they were busted. But he never said anything, so I knew he was playing. Hell, he only missed one game in his entire career. And that was before I was coach, and he cried because they wouldn't let him in. He would never ask out of a game. You would have to cut his leg off for that to happen. Kurt Becker, one of our offensive linemen, was bruised pretty bad. Covert had no feeling in his right arm. Maybe a pinched nerve, who knew? Dennis McKinnon had a hip pointer, and he was still recovering from that offseason knee surgery. But he was a tough son of a bitch, too. He never said anything about pain, but I knew what a hip pointer was. I had one in college, and I played with it and the muscle slipped off the edge and down into my abdomen. You keep playing with it, and you get injections, and when the painkillers wear off, it hurts so much you can't cough, you can't fart, you can barely sit.

The weird thing Dennis did, though, was he started talking about the Vikings. "I don't think they're as good as their record says," he said. Bulletin-board crap. Now I don't advocate stuff like that. But if you can back it up, I guess it's okay. And I wouldn't change anything about Dennis. I loved him.

We go up to Minneapolis on Wednesday because of the league's rule about being at the opposing site 24 hours in advance. This is a place I don't like, especially just three days after our last game. Guys are definitely sore and hurting. McMahon doesn't practice. Now he's saying he thinks he hurt his back sleeping on his *waterbed* a week earlier. His waterbed. And he says he doesn't need to practice at all, all he needs is to know the game plan and different formations. The media keeps asking me if McMahon is going to start. And I'm getting pissed off, and now I realize I actually want Fuller in there. He beat the Vikings the year before 34-3 when we clinched the division. He threw for two touchdowns. I'd like to show that he, Steve Fuller—and we—can do it again without McMahon at quarterback. So everybody shut up and sit down. Steve Fuller is my guy.

The game started, and the noise in that damn roller rink was a real pain. I hate the Metrodome. But the hell with it. There was a bigger problem. We were getting our asses handed to us.

The offense was sputtering along, doing nothing. I could see that Walter was not himself. And all of the time we were falling behind, McMahon was bugging the shit out of me. He was pouting down on the bench, then he was standing behind me, then he was following me around like a puppy. I turned around and almost stepped on top of him. "Put me in," he was saying. "I can play. I'm fine."

He was driving me crazy! We hadn't practiced on Monday, then on Tuesday we were in shorts, no pads. We hadn't changed much in our game plan, because there was no time. This is what we do, and the coaches can't get pregnant with ideas. And Jim knew this. Get away from me! I'm thinking. But he's right there like a mosquito, just pestering me to death.

At halftime we're down 10-6. Then in the third quarter we close it to 10-9 on another Butler field goal, but Vikings quarterback Tommy Kramer throws a TD pass, and they're up, 17-9. All we've gotten after seven drives into their territory are three Butthead field goals. It isn't Fuller's fault, but things just aren't clicking.

"I can do it," McMahon is saying. He's driving me absolutely nuts.

Headband buddies Wally and Mac were the soul and heart of our offense.
Jonathan Daniel/Getty Images

"You can't throw the ball!" I say to him. "And you know you can't."

"You gotta put me in," he keeps saying. "I can throw."

"How can I put you in? You haven't practiced."

But he did go through warmups. I don't know how. But he did. That much was true.

"Put me in."

"I don't want you getting hurt all over again."

I wanted to win with Fuller. I thought about how we'd had to do it without McMahon before, and we'd probably have to again. I wanted to show we could do it for me, too. To prove to myself I didn't need him, that as a team, we really didn't need anybody.

Jim keeps standing beside me, then in front of me. Yapping away. The game's going on, and I'm trying to coach.

"Shut up!" I say. "We're trying to win!"

Then the third quarter's half over, and our ass is up against the wall. He's like a little rat terrier, biting my ankle.

"Okay," I say. "You're in."

I call a play, and I don't remember what it was, but McMahon gets to the line and I can tell he's calling an audible. Jesus. He's calling out "Blue-69," which is a weak side takeoff for Willie Gault, a fly route.

Now the thing about McMahon is he has the uncanny ability to recognize a blitz just by reading the defense. He could look at a safety and know what was coming just from the safety's alignment, just from his eyes, just from his attitude and body language. So Willie takes off on the left side, and here comes the blitz. There was no way we could pick it up with our blocking. So Payton nails one guy really good and then he takes just a piece out of the other guy. It was like bumper pool. McMahon's falling back, and at the last second he heaves the ball and, my God, it's a perfect pass and Willie catches it for a 70-yard touchdown.

One play. Insane. The Vikings *knew* he couldn't throw. That's what I thought, too. But he did.

Then we get the ball back, and McMahon goes in, and on the first play throws a 25-yard touchdown pass to McKinnon. Two plays, 95 yards passing, two touchdowns. I can't believe it. I have no idea how he's doing it. They are blitzing the crap out of him because they didn't think he could throw. They *knew* he couldn't throw, and they knew his two touchdowns had to be luck. And then he throws *another* touchdown! This one a 43-yarder to McKinnon.

These are the busted-up Bears, remember? Are we tough? What do you think? McKinnon is just one of the guys who is playing hurt. I'll tell you something about him. There was a game in 1987 when we were playing the Giants at Soldier Field and I was sick of Lawrence Taylor coming off the line like he was running a 40-yard dash with track spikes on and a hot babe at the finish line. I called McKinnon aside and told him he was going to come in motion from the outside toward the tight end, and he was going to be set up on Taylor for a strong side block. "And you're going to knock the shit out of him!" I added. L.T. went about 250 pounds and might have been the best defensive end or whatever he was, ever. Dennis went maybe 185, and his legs were beat and his arms were frail. You know what McKinnon said? "Okay." That simple.

He came in on a jog, then squared up and just sold out and hit Taylor as hard as he could and sent him flying. L.T. got up and looked at me on the sideline and yelled, "Ditka, you're an asshole!"

"What? I'm gonna let you run around and make every tackle?" I yelled back. "Watch out now. This guy's got balls and he's coming after you!"

Taylor's head was on a swivel the whole afternoon, and we negated his effectiveness. Dennis did, that is.

So anyway, back in the Minnesota game it's still the third quarter, five minutes have gone by, and this crazy McMahon has thrown for three touchdowns and we're ahead 30-17.

We won the game 33-24, Jim was the star of the hour, and I couldn't have been happier with that scrawny McKinnon, either. Payton said, "It was like everybody came in at halftime and got out their rosary beads."

I couldn't have prayed for anything like that. But what I was thinking was that if it hadn't been for our offensive line, none of this would have happened. If Walter hadn't hit those two blitzers, it wouldn't have happened. But here we are, and it did happen. I know we wouldn't have won that game without McMahon. We wouldn't have won the Super Bowl without him.

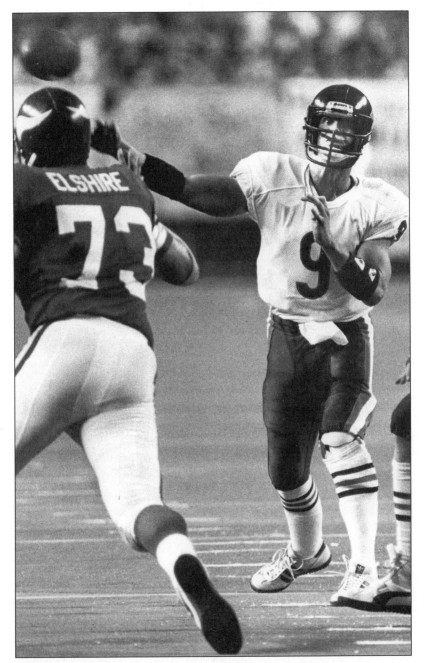

McMahon could throw any way he wanted—even from left field.
Jonathan Daniel/Getty Images

I had wanted to prove some stuff to myself, but I had to back off and admit I was wrong. Joe Namath and all those ABC guys were there, and now the Bears were a big deal. Like I said, I didn't read the papers, but sometimes people told me what was going on. It was nothing new for me. The good guys were still good guys, and the assholes were still assholes. I mean, *Tribune* columnist Bernie Lincicome was still a jerk, what can I tell you? Writers started bugging me just to see what kind of a response they'd get. Sometimes I didn't handle it very well, but there are times when there isn't a good answer at all. *Do you still cheat on your wife?* I mean, help me out here.

I went on Channel 2 one time, and what's her name, Diann Burns, asked me a question, and I just flat out told her, "That's not a good question." Especially after a game, I needed a little time to come down, to cool the burners. I was better on Mondays than Sundays. Better Wednesdays than Mondays.

I'm not defending my behavior. Could I have handled things better in my career, like when I jumped all over Avellini or Harbaugh or yelled at reporters? Sure. But I handled it the way I knew how, and that's why I can't go back and apologize to anybody. McMahon called me Sybil, I've heard. Well, screw it—I didn't care what anybody said about me. I've always maintained that if your job isn't important to you, then don't do it. And my Bears job meant everything to me. I cared about what people said about my team, not me. It bothered me when I heard writers were writing bad stuff about the guys. I always felt like I was defending the entire history of the franchise.

I hate losing. I just do. Some things I can't win at. You want to challenge me in ballet or nuclear physics, you're going to whip my ass. But not in football. Not my Bears. Because I can do something about that.

It was like the season before, during the week leading up to the NFC championship game against the 49ers. The front-office guys wanted to redo my contract and sign me for another three years or something. I said, "Not now. We're coming up against the biggest game the Bears have had in years." It wasn't so I could negotiate better later. It was that I wanted no distractions. Michael McCaskey, the president, didn't seem to have a clue about that. He said, "I really want to announce it to the team, let them know you're going to be the coach for a long time."

I said, "They don't give a shit about that. They just want to play football."

Why was that so hard to understand?

We got whipped anyway. But I truly wasn't concerned about the contract or security at that time. All I wanted to do was make the Old Man proud. Make myself proud. Not make New Man McCaskey proud.

Now there was less time to think about any of that outside stuff. We were 3-0, and looking solid. I liked the fact that our offense had now bailed out our great defense in two of the three games. That made me feel good. I guess part of it was my competition with Buddy, my desire to make him know that our side of the ball was as valuable as his.

I was also glad we had 10 days off before we played the Redskins at home. We could use the time to heal, and I knew some of the guys could use the time to party a little bit.

McMahon probably wanted to party, but by the next day he was back in his favorite spot, the Lake Forest Hospital. Now besides his bad back, he had an infected leg bruise. He was in traction, and he had this lower leg thing that was getting treated with heat and antibiotics and elevation. The doc thought Jim might have gotten the infection from a hand cut during an exhibition game.

I was beginning to think that waking up each morning was a dangerous thing for this reckless guy. Whatever. The Bears were now on the map. And after his game in Minneapolis, Jim McMahon was near the center of it all.

Chapter Seven

Yolanda Is Waiting, Meester Deetka

Dexter Manley, the Washington Redskins' unpredictable and loud-mouthed defensive end, said early in the week that even though quarterback Jim McMahon was a threat on offense, Walter Payton's running was more of a trouble spot for the 'Skins. "We're gonna have to knock Walter Payton out of the game," Manley said sweetly. "We're gonna have to do that." Not bad logic, perhaps. But not genius, either. And definitely not good pregame hype.

The entire Bears team was studded with special athletes, special personalities. Payton was, indeed, the most special of them all. The wily running back out of little Jackson State was now in his 11th NFL year, and he desperately wanted a championship ring before his time ran out. He had been the leading scorer in NCAA history when he left college, but he knew he needed to make his mark on the big stage, the NFL, to leave a truly grand legacy. In 1984 he had played in his seventh Pro Bowl, but he had been on mostly mediocre teams this far in his career with the Bears—and that was why getting so close to the Super Bowl the year before had pained him so much. Time waits for no one. And as a not-so-big (five-foot-11, 205-pound), workhorse tailback who had already carried the ball over 3,000 times in his pro career—Walter's clock was ticking fast.

A bigger problem for the Redskins, however, was their own record. They were 1-2 and had been wiped out in their season opener against the Cowboys 44-14 with quarterback Joe Theismann throwing five interceptions. Just the previous week they had nearly blown a 16-0 lead over the Houston Oilers before squeaking out a 16-13 win.

The Bears had beaten the Redskins 23-19 in last year's playoff first round, but it had not been easy. Indeed, the Redskins had taken an intentional safety in the fourth quarter of that game, just on the chance of getting the ball back in better field position for a final run at a victory. The gamble failed, but the intent was there. Ditka was not complacent or certain about this fourth game. He

worried about a blabbermouth like Manley, but most of all he
worried about a shrewd coach like Washington's Joe Gibbs.

Any time you play a Joe Gibbs-coached team, you worry. You know there's a lot going on in that mind, and you know he's thinking about stopping you. Joe retired years later, after winning the Super Bowl a couple times. Then he went on to be a car owner in NASCAR, and then I guess he got bored, because he came back to the NFL in 2004. Right now he hasn't done too well with the Redskins in his second stint. But I think he'll get it together. You don't get stupid fast.

A season or so later, I said Manley had the IQ of a grapefruit. That was a dumb thing to say, but I didn't need to hear him flapping his mouth all the time. Hell, he had his own problems with drugs and other stuff, anyway. A columnist in Chicago said Manley "had the biggest mouth in a city of politicians," so that was about all you needed to know. And I was going to stand up for my guys against everyone, take the heat for them. When you're a team, it's like you're actually all part of the same person. If I took the heat, so what?

The thing that happened in the Washington game was that it got away from the Redskins real fast. Sometimes that happens when nobody expects it. They had a guy, Jeff Hayes, who was their kicker and punter, and he pulled a thigh muscle kicking off after they first scored, and that just ruined them. Willie Gault took off after he caught the kickoff, made some fakes, turned on the jets, and ran right past Hayes for a 99-yard touchdown to put us up 10-7. It was the beginning of the second quarter, and by halftime we were up 31-10. Thirty-one points in a quarter is pretty big. Let people say what they wanted about our offense. You go get 31 points in 15 minutes.

Right away Washington had to punt, and I wondered who they'd put back there, and this is wonderful, because it's

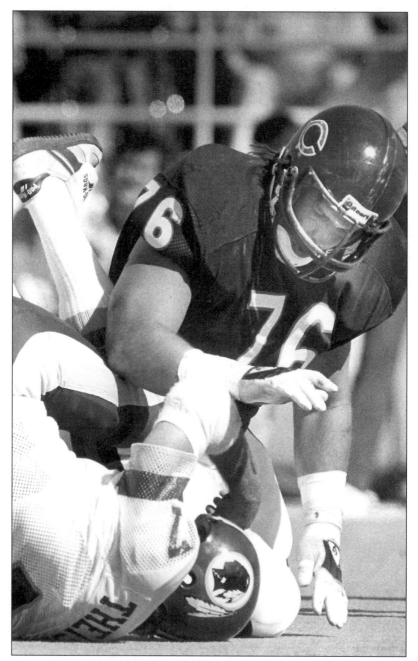

Steve McMichael is asking Joe Theismann if he needs help getting his knee out of his mouth. *Jonathan Daniel/Getty Images*

Theismann. I'm thinking, "Look at that! That punt's gonna go *behind* him!" When the ball was finished doing whatever it was doing in the air, then on the ground, it actually netted one yard. After that their backup quarterback, Jay Schroeder, punted. But it was over. We destroyed Washington 45-10, their worst defeat in 24 years.

If you look at the stats from that game, they're deceptive. We only had 16 first downs and just 250 net yards on offense. They had 19 first downs and 376 net yards. And you know what? They did stop Payton. He only carried the ball seven times and gained six yards. But we were at our best, because we were opportunistic.

McMahon had recovered fairly well from his injuries—I mean at least he was upright and not in a body cast—and he came into the game almost like a real, non-limping quarterback. So you want to stop Walter, huh? Fine. Jimmy Mac hands him the ball and the whole Redskins team goes after Wally, and—*la ti da*—there goes Mac up the other sideline. Nobody's on him, because why should you care about a beat-up quarterback like him? He just jogs away from everybody like he's looking back, watching the play.

But Payton stops suddenly and throws a perfect spiral back across the field to McMahon, who runs in untouched for a 13-yard TD. That made it 28-10. Who cares if it's the wide receiver who scores on a pass or the quarterback? People can say we were fortunate in that game, but we made our own fortune. Where was grapefruit Manley when Payton threw the ball?

The thing is, Walter was such a great football player that you could do things with him that you couldn't with other backs. I think he could throw a football 70 yards. Hell, you think that touchdown pass to McMahon was his first in the NFL? It was his eighth! And he could punt. He did that for us a couple times in games. He could kick off. In college he kicked

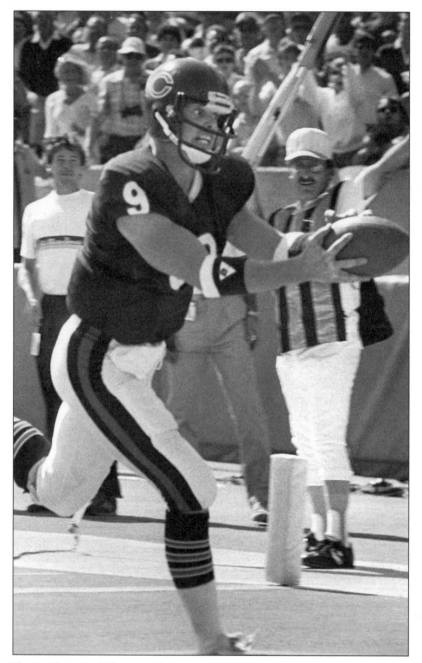

The Redskins should have paid more attention to the quarterback, who's catching a TD pass from Walter Payton. *Jonathan Daniel/Getty Images*

five field goals and over 50 extra points. When we really got busted up in one season, I even had him play at quarterback.

So far this season his stats weren't great—even though he caught a 33-yard touchdown pass from McMahon later in the Redskins game—but we were winning. And his potential was always there. He could be the greatest decoy ever made. Think how much that helps a team. So far he had only 50 carries for 227 yards, which computed to about a 900-yard season. And he'd already had eight 1,000-yard seasons. He only missed going over 1,000 in his rookie year and in 1982, when there was a strike. But he had that pride that you couldn't kill. Nobody worked harder than he did getting in shape. He was the best conditioned athlete on our team. He was like a rock. If he had any fat on him, you couldn't have grabbed it with pliers. He'd run that hill of his down in Mississippi, and I think he had a hill here in the Chicago suburbs, and he'd leave guys who were trying to stay with him half-dead, puking their guts out at the bottom.

In games after every run, he'd push the ball forward a few inches. The ref would move it back, but maybe over the course of his career Walter gained 50 yards that way. He had that high step, too. When he was breaking away from tacklers, he'd lift his legs up like a drum major. He did that in college, too. It was like his trademark. Some people may have thought he was hotdogging, but he never was a showboat, a hot dog, nothing. Never. You gotta have a little dislike for the other team, but you have to have respect, too, and I think Walter had the perfect mix. He respected all those guys trying to crush him, but he wanted them to know that the forearm to their chest or stiff arm right in their mouth was to prove they weren't bringing him down.

I mean, how big a heart did this guy have? The year before in the Washington game I said, "It's gonna be rough, Walter. We're not blocking them very well."

He said, "Coach, just keep giving it to me. We'll pound 'em."

"I don't want you hurt," I said.

"They can't hurt me," he said. "I'm watching them. They can't hurt me."

He ran like a madman in that game. When we lost the next week to the 49ers in the NFC game, Walter was devastated. He was limping pretty bad afterward. A reporter asked him if he was hurt. "Not on the outside," he said.

Walter and I talked at times. But we didn't talk a lot. I'll tell you the truth—there wasn't a whole lot to coach there. He was a complete football player. He knew everything, and if he didn't know, he'd just ask Suhey. Matt lined up in front of him a lot, to block—that's how Walter grabbed his shorts and his jock strap that one time—and anything Walter didn't understand about a play, Matt would tell him. They had a great relationship. It was one of those really important relationships built on trust and having proved yourself to the other guy. Football teams, good ones, are full of small trusts like that. When they all come together, that's when you have a great team.

Take that Washington game. Yeah, they had guys injured and they lost their punter. But we had three starters out, too. Including Covert at left tackle. That's a pretty important position. But Andy Frederick came in and did a great job.

Now don't get me wrong about Payton. He sure as hell wasn't all serious and quiet. Everybody knows that. I didn't mind guys having their own personalities. God knows I was no altar boy when I was a player, and I didn't want a bunch of clones. But there was only one Walter, no matter what. Off the field he was beloved by the fans. I never once saw him say no to somebody looking for an autograph, to kids, to old folks, to the real people, anyway, not those frauds looking to get autographs and sell them. And he was a practical joker. If there was an explosion, you knew it was Walter. If a firework went off anywhere, anytime, you knew it was him. All kinds of stuff. He busted my balls all the time, and sometimes it was really good.

I remember I'd be in my office late at night and I'd get these phone calls. There'd be this Latino woman on the other end, and she had a thick Mexican accent and a real high voice and she'd say, "Meester Deetka, I am Yolanda. I am very *caliente* and I want to meet you at the motel down the street. I'm waiting for you! Please come, *señor!*"

I got these calls all the time, and then about a month later I found out it was Walter. I saw him at practice and I said, "You little prick!" God, he thought it was funny.

Now so many years later, I still think about him and what a tragedy it was when he died. It was only 1999, and he was still young. He was always so strong and healthy; it was just mind-blowing to see him wasted away. He used to have a grip that was unreal, bring you to your knees. But what that liver cancer did to him was terrible. I never dreamed he'd be the first one to go from that team—before even any coaches. My offensive coordinator Ed Hughes died in 2000, and that was sad. But *Walter?* Going *first?* I remember a team doctor once told me early on that Payton's blood enzymes were a little screwed up, but what did that mean? It was no big deal. How could it be?

It just hurts for me to remember him being ill, losing his body that way. I spoke at his funeral, but I hate funerals. I want to celebrate life. I want to celebrate Walter Payton's life. He left a great wife, Connie, and their two wonderful kids. Man, he was a fun guy, I'm telling you.

And in 1985, he was obviously the guy who made our offense work. When I first took over in 1982, Buddy's defense

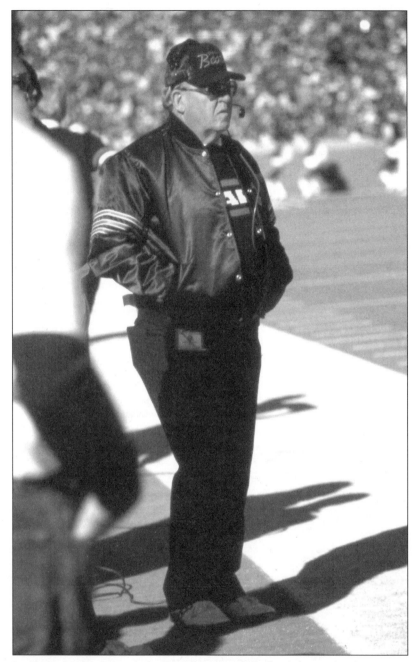

Buddy and I sometimes clashed, but he was a hell of a defensive leader.
Photo by Vernon J. Biever

seemed to just want to beat up our offense all the time. I'll say that again and again, because it's true. There were defensive players who didn't even know the names of the guys on offense. Didn't *want* to know. What good was that going to do for Walter? For all of us? Finally, I told Buddy that the Bears were not on our schedule. I guess I said that a few times through the early years. And now we had become a single unit—or at least the defense respected us. And knew our fricking *names*. Especially Payton's.

And why not? We already had scored 136 points, more than anybody in the league. We needed to keep our consistency and togetherness. It bothered the defense a lot that Bell and Harris were apparently not coming back. And now Richard Dent was making noise about being underpaid. He'd made the Pro Bowl in 1984, just his second season, and he *was* underpaid at $90,000 a year. But we didn't need him asking to get traded, saying stuff like, "Maybe I can play somewhere else," right during the thick of things. Next year, maybe. Nah, not even then—just get it done in the offseason. Later on I called him Robert Dent, kind of as a joke. I probably shouldn't have done it—but it was a joke, people! Anyway, it was just my way of saying let's all keep pulling together, and nobody's name is that important. He wanted more publicity, so I gave it to him. But a Super Bowl ring is what it's all about, isn't it? Hell yes, it is. Already people were saying our offensive success was because of Jim McMahon and had nothing to do with me. Fine, I'll put that aside. Let's just keep rolling.

Things were going on around us, but I was oblivious. I think people don't realize how coaches are, how narrow they make their world. Look, I knew that John McEnroe was playing good tennis. And I knew Michael Jordan was this young kid for the Bulls, and he was starting his second season and he was amazing, but that was it. I look back and see that the Cubs

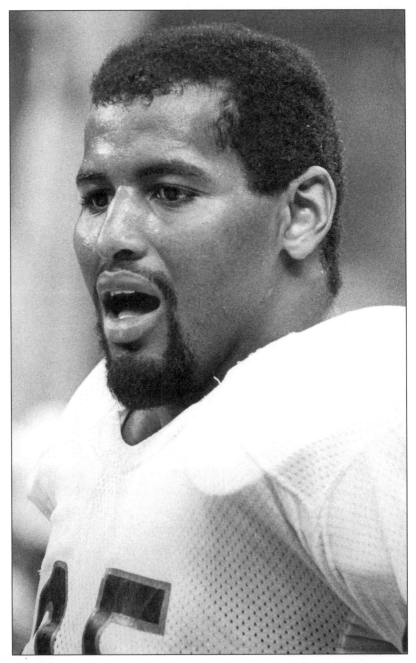

Robert Dent, excuse me, Richard Dent—the deserving Super Bowl MVP.
Photo by Vernon J. Biever

couldn't get lights for night games at Wrigley Field. The Illinois Supreme Court said forget it. Of course, this was 20 years before Bob Thomas would run the court. Who knows what he would have ruled?

But I knew nothing about any of it, and I didn't care. It's pretty funny to see what Cubs president Dallas Green said. He was mad and said nobody would help the Cubs until it was crisis time, "And it will be crisis time next year when we have to play the playoffs and World Series in St. Louis." Well, they didn't have to worry about that, did they? No, the Cubs are pretty consistent about not going all the way.

We had Tampa Bay to get ready for again. There wasn't a whole lot of news, except that everything we did seemed to get magnified in Chicago. William Perry weighed in at his semi-weekly weigh-in, and he was a sleek 314 pounds. That was down from 330 in training camp, and hip-hip-hooray! He made 1,000 bucks, or something like that, every time he was under 315. The Fridge was unloaded! I remember later when he was getting really heavy, and he would tell me how he wasn't eating anything at all during the day. And he wasn't. But at night he might eat enough for five people. But he was a slender fellow in 1985, folks. He was a swizzle stick.

The Bucs game was a lousy one. We went down there and fell behind by 12 points and looked like crap. But Payton ran for two touchdowns, and we pulled it out 27-19. A win is a lot better than a loss, but Tampa Bay was 0-5, so how good could we feel? Buddy wasn't using Perry all that much on defense, and some media people—following Buddy's lead—were saying he was a wasted draft pick. I sure didn't think so. He was fat. But underneath all that stuff was a hell of an athlete. I had seen how fast he was off the ball for a few yards, and I knew he could dunk a basketball. So we put ol' Fridge on the kickoff coverage team, and darned if he didn't make two tackles. Tampa Bay

Down in Tampa Bay, I'm clean, neat, and feisty. The Bucs would be victims, and we would be 5-0. *Jonathan Daniel/Getty Images*

blockers weren't exactly thrilled to see this giant appliance rumbling their way.

The bigger issue was that we'd been forced to come from behind in several of our games, and maybe that wasn't a good sign. But maybe, too, it meant we could beat people even when we weren't playing our best.

We'd find out soon. We were undefeated. But we traveled to San Francisco in six days, to play the world-champion San Francisco 49ers. We remembered them quite well.

Chapter Eight

Sic 'Em Fridge, and the Premature Celebration

All week long 49ers coach Bill Walsh praised the Bears, saying their offense was "exceptionally well-designed," and basically magnificent and untouchable, and their defense "was possibly the most effective defense in football." Ditka was even more congratulatory and effusive, difficult as that might seem. The Bears coach came close to fainting, his bodice was so tight. San Francisco had "the most intimidating defense I've ever seen," he said. And it had "the most innovative offense that's ever been." Ditka didn't say he thought Bill Walsh was God, but it might have been on his mind. Ditka hoped against hope that his Bears wouldn't get "blown out of the city." Gentlemen, grab your barf bags.

Ever the man with an intuitive grasp of the absurd, Ditka told newsmen he had even considered calling NFL commissioner Pete Rozelle. "What if we both didn't show up?" he asked.

San Francisco, though 3-2, still had the highest rating in the silly Dunkel NFL Index, but the Bears were No. 3, right behind the runner-up Miami Dolphins. "Did they announce it yet?" Ditka said at his Thursday press conference. "The game's been cancelled. Mutual fear."

But the rematch of the NFC championship game contenders was on. Same field. Same coaches. But one team had a different quarterback. Jim McMahon. And Ditka himself was certain he had learned from the embarrassing defeat the season before.

Fans at that January NFC title game out in San Francisco had been screaming at us, "When you come back, bring an offense!" It was a fair thing to yell. I had thought we could play conservatively, hang around, and win with our defense in that game. I found out we couldn't. So we came ready to roll this time. We wanted the other team to be intimidated. We wanted to establish some fear if we could. Lots of it.

This was our offense, doing things right. Walter came out and he was pumped up, to say the least. He rushed for 132

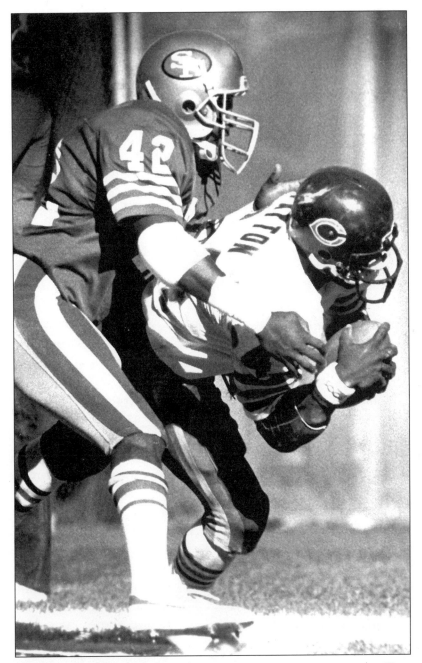

Walter takes Ronnie Lott into the end zone in our revenge game against the 49ers.
Jonathan Daniel/Getty Images

yards and he scored two touchdowns. The last one, in the fourth quarter, he carried two 49ers around the left end with him right into the end zone. It was a 17-yard sweep and it put us up 26-10, and that was the final score.

We played without Dennis McKinnon and tight end Emery Moorehead, because they were injured, and used backups Ken Margerum and Tim Wrightman to fill in. They did fine. Hell, we scored the first four times we had the ball. Our offensive line was exploding off the ball and blocking like crazy. And, of course, our great defense was there. I don't think Walsh and his guys knew what hit them. Joe Montana was sacked seven times, the most in his career, and they only got 183 net yards, not even half their average.

Like I said, we had a big chip on our shoulder from the year before. Payton told the press afterward that the 49ers hadn't shown us much "courtesy or dignity" when they beat us before, and also that they said "negative things about our offense." That made me smile a little. But we already had gotten the last laugh.

We had that 26-10 lead, and our defense had stopped them again, naturally, and we were running out the clock to end the game. Well, let's pause for a moment.

I remembered when Walsh put that big load McIntyre in the backfield the year before, and how I didn't much appreciate it. Plus, I like to be a little—what do you want to call it?—creative? So I called Fridge over, and we had a little conference. He was at attention and was like, "Okay, Coach! Yessir, Coach!" I told him to go in and tell McMahon he was running the ball. Just grab the ball, hold it like a sack of money, and head south. We hadn't practiced Fridge running or put anything in the play book about it. But the guys might have had an idea I was going to try something different. Perry went thundering off at full speed, screaming to the ref that he was reporting to the backfield and yelling to McMahon that he was now a running back. I didn't know what Buddy was thinking about this, but what the hell. If the defense isn't going to use this guy, I'm gonna. I knew Bill Walsh would appreciate it.

So McMahon gave Perry the ball, and Fridge crashed straight into the line. Our offensive linemen were terrified he might fall on them. Hilgenberg used a cut block on his man just to get down and out of the way. We gave the ball to Fridge on the next play, too, and it was just another huge collision. I don't think the defenders knew what the hell was happening. I know they weren't crazy about tackling Big Bill. Their safety Carlton Williamson said afterward he personally was "a little upset about it."

Hey, screw 'em! It's football. If you can kick somebody's ass, shouldn't you do it? It was revenge for me. Yeah, I'll admit it. A little bit. Maybe a lot. Even though my first thought about using Fridge back there was this big fellow can really block. I'd watch him in sprints in practice, and for the first five yards or so there was all this dirt flying up from under his shoes. Looked like a roto-tiller. I didn't like it when they used McIntyre in the backfield against us, that's for sure. So here's a response.

Buddy had his favorites, which is okay, because he was one of those old coaches who believes you have to earn your spurs, and that rookies generally can't play. He really believed players had to earn the right to be out there. Being the first draft choice, like Perry, meant nothing to him. But Buddy was dead wrong about Perry and his abilities. Buddy didn't even want us to draft him. He called him "Fatso" or just "Number 72." Fine, I'll take the big kid. And I did.

The problem was Buddy saw this as a slap in the face. That wasn't how I meant it. It just made us a better football team, I thought. Okay, and it was fun. I guarantee you goal-line practices became a lot more fun with Fridge back there. And I started thinking of other things to do with him. Back then, remember, a huge player was like 275 pounds. Three-fourteen? Three-thirty? It was crazy.

So now we are all the rage. We *are* the sideshow. It had been building, and the Minnesota game got everybody's attention, and McMahon and Payton and Singletary were pretty well known. But this was big. In four days we're going to be on the cover of *Sports Illustrated*. Well, McMahon was on it, throwing a pass over a San Francisco player, above the headline, "BEARS ON THE PROWL: Jim McMahon Leads Undefeated Chicago Past the 49ers."

I felt pretty good. I felt I had redeemed our team from the embarrassment of the year before. Well, they had done it. I am certain we had more talent than anybody. But talent doesn't always win. The sideshow stuff didn't affect me; it wasn't important to me. I wanted to be proud of being a coach for this team and city I loved. You only get a few opportunities in life; that's it, and you better grab them.

A lot of people thought it was nuts when I was hired to coach the team. But when Mr. Halas hired me, he didn't hire me for Xs and Os. He hired me because I was a *Bear*. His own family didn't have anybody like me in it. They weren't football people. The McCaskeys didn't play. I think Halas hired me because he had a gut instinct, and he followed it. When I first arrived, he asked me what I wanted to do for my staff, if I had people in mind.

"I have a few," I said.

Then he said, "I would really like you to keep the defensive coaches."

"Why?" I said.

"Because that's a very strong part of our football team. Buddy Ryan came here in 1978, and the players like him and they play hard for him."

"Fine," I said. "I have no problem at all with that."

I meant it.

I only brought in a couple of coaches, mainly Ed Hughes, whom I'd been with for a few years in Dallas, to be offensive coordinator. Buddy was a hell of a coach. But I know he thought he should have been named head coach. There was nothing I could do about that. You have to understand that when I first got there, the Bears defense was much, much better than the offense. We had to build the offense little by little, put the pieces of the puzzle in place. But it was hard to do when we were practicing against those guys and they were going full speed and we couldn't accomplish anything. They were better than us, cut and dried. Understand? So what? Buddy and I would have the argument constantly, over and over and over. *We don't play the Bears, Buddy. I don't see them on our schedule. Do you? Where? We have to play the other team's defense, not ours!* The attitude and respect changed after Covert body-slammed McMichael. And after Fridge played against San Francisco, too. But still I had to tell Buddy to put William in on defense. I mean, this guy was a good athlete. He didn't deserve the rap of being just a fat guy, and he sure as hell wasn't lazy.

I wanted Buddy to know we could not win if we had different goals. The only goal should be the whole team's success. But I saw him get caught up in stats and sacks and stuff like that. I mean, why were we blitzing when we're up 21 points? Because we're the No. 1-rated defense and we want more sacks. So I was going to use one of his defensive players when I wanted to.

And I felt good and celebrated just a bit after our win. We got on the plane, and I started drinking wine with Jerry Vainisi. I mean, it wasn't like we were crazy celebrating. I was just relishing the little bit we'd accomplished. It's a long flight from California, and the wine kept coming. We felt good and we were dissecting the game, enjoying the glow. When we got to

O'Hare early in the morning, everybody went scrambling for their cars. I got in mine and took off and headed north on I-294.

All of a sudden I see a police light turn on, and the next thing I know, I pull over and the guy is giving me a ticket for driving under the influence. I was wrong, and driving after drinking is a terrible thing. But the guy was a prick. I was 100 percent wrong, I admit that. But here I am on the side of the highway, and players are flying past in their cars and they're looking at their coach getting arrested. I think a player or two stopped, and I told them to keep on going. I didn't think I was drunk. My judgment was good, but maybe it wasn't perfect. I argue with that cop, call him everything I can think of. Everything in the book. It's not a good scene.

I did everything I was supposed to do, though I didn't take a breathalyzer, because I didn't want to. Tom Landry called me during the week, and I appreciated that. We talked all the time, anyway, but he just called to give me support. He told the press I was a "good man," and that was nice.

I came in and gave a talk to the players on Monday, apologizing to them, to the organization, for my behavior. They needed to forgive me, and I didn't need my authority undercut. And we sure didn't need any more distractions on our road to the postseason. So I wanted to get this all behind me.

Some press guy told Darryl Rogers, the Detroit Lions head coach, what I'd done, and Darryl said, "I guess I'd probably do that, too."

Darryl doesn't drink. And the press guy reminded him he didn't drink, in case he'd forgotten.

"But I would if we were 6-0," said Darryl.

Yes, we were still undefeated. And it was Packer week. And nobody who calls himself a Chicago Bear can relax during Packer week. I know I didn't.

Chapter Nine

Hit Lists in Cheeseland, the Marvelous Mudslide, Halfway Home

The Green Bay Packers and Bears have played, as of this writing, 168 times. The two teams are separated by about 175 miles, many different heroes, villains, successes, failures, and—as Wisconsinites will quickly remind those from down south—the Illinois state line. That border, their T-shirts will tell you, is the difference between "a Cheesehead and a ----head." Being in the NFC Central and vying for the same title year after year since George Halas and Curly Lambeau were young men have made the battles between Green Bay and Chicago especially spirited. If that's the word. Hate comes to mind. Or at least it did when Ditka's teams played.

The Bears of 1985 were already a major success. They were undefeated, of course. But now they were becoming more of an attraction, a media fascination, a variety show, so to speak. They were something new in the sports field, entertainment in and of themselves, complete and self-contained. All they needed was the random foe. Ditka would never put it that way. He worried as he coached. But this first Packers game of the season was in Chicago, on the shores of Lake Michigan, at artificial turf-clad Soldier Field, and that soothed him some. It was a homecoming of sorts, because the Bears had been on the road the last two games. And it was the team's first foray of the season into the fiery-hot glare of ABC's monumentally rated Monday Night Football. *The scene was set for something dramatic—or at least melodramatic—to happen. Ditka would never let folks down.*

Now, you have to understand I don't hate the Packers. The Old Man had tried to instill that in me, hatred, he tried to drum it in to me. But I never hated the Packers. I never wanted to kill them or see them as mortal enemies. I respected those players, because I knew that they were part of a great organization, one of the best, as far as I'm concerned. At least under Lombardi they sure were. I never really disliked anybody up there. Respect is important, more than hatred. I never even disliked the Green Bay fans. They always treated me pretty well, even with all of the booing. They could get on me at Lambeau Field pretty damn good, but this game was at Soldier Field, our home.

If there was an issue at all, it was that we wanted to go all the way this year, and Green Bay was a roadblock in our path. Also, their coach was Forrest Gregg, a guy I'd played against when he was with the Packers and I was with the Bears, and I knew him pretty well.

I liked Forrest Gregg. I mean I never disliked him. Didn't hate him. But the year before, in the preseason, we were playing them up in Milwaukee at the Shriner's Game thing, and they were going to win the game—I mean, it's just August and we're looking at different players—and he did some stuff at the end of the game I didn't appreciate. The game was over, for all intents and purposes, and they were trying to score or something—why I don't know—and I told the press afterward that it was stupid, that he was stupid, that all that could happen was somebody would get hurt doing this stupid crap.

I know I was wrong to say anything. It was football. But he got pissed off at me, and then I got pissed off at him, and it lingered through all of 1984. But this game was important. Just to win, the hell with Forrest Gregg. Here was the thing. During the week I actually put in plays for William Perry at fullback, plays we practiced. I had already used him as a runner to kill the clock, and the world went nuts. Let's see how the world liked having him block, too. And, hmm, what about this mammoth guy, the guy Hampton had nicknamed "Biscuit"—because he was a biscuit over 350 in training camp—actually scoring? Fridge, the touchdown-maker. I liked the concept.

We started out like crap, fumbling three times, and the Packers took the lead 7-0. It was the second quarter and we finally started to move, getting down to the Green Bay two-yard line. I yelled, "William, get in there!" Out Perry rumbles, and the *Monday Night* crowd goes bananas. He lined up over right tackle and he made the lead block for Walter. He hit Packers linebacker George Cumby and he just, I don't know, *absorbed* the poor guy. Cumby weighed 90 pounds less than Fridge, and he took him on high and, my God, I thought they'd end up in Indiana. Walter scored like it was nothing, like he was eating an apple at a picnic.

Not long after that we got down to the goal line again, and I signaled for Fridge to get out there. He went out and lined up behind right tackle, as usual. But this time Jim handed him the ball. Fridge charged into the blockers and dove across the goal line like I guess he'd seen Walter do before. I thought the end zone would tilt. I mean this guy has a 22-inch neck, wears a size 58 coat. He could bench 465. Ray Sons wrote after the game in the *Sun-Times* that it was "the best use of fat since the invention of bacon."

Now the crowd is truly nuts. I can tell the difference in the sound. Perry has turned the game around, and football fans everywhere are watching and enjoying this. Call it a sideshow; I called it beating their ass. Think about it. How would *you* stop a man that size coming directly at you?

With a little more than a minute left in the half, we get down to the goal line one more time. I fiddle around and send in a couple of other substitutes. Everybody is chanting, "Per-ree! Per-ree!" I know what they want, but let's tease this for just a second. What the hell, it's entertainment, isn't it? *Okay, Fridge, get on out there!* Now McMahon is waving his arms in circles, getting the roaring crowd even more into it. Perry lines up on the other side this time, just for the variation, over left tackle, and I can see poor Cumby is across from him once again. He has to follow because of their defensive scheme or whatever.

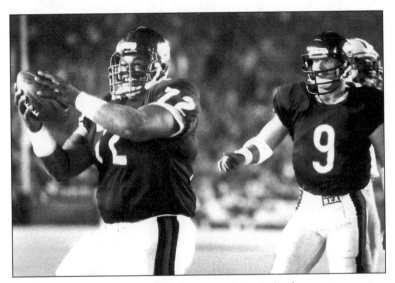

I think McMahon is telling Fridge not to hurt the ball after scoring against Green Bay. *Jonathan Daniel/Getty Images*

Mac gives the ball to Payton, who follows behind Fridge, who obliterates Cumby once more.

"I felt like I was stealing," is what Walter said afterward about the touchdown. Cumby said something about how he thought about taking on one side of Perry, but it didn't matter because "one side is as big as another."

We were ahead 21-7, and a legend was being built. We went on to win 23-7 after Otis Wilson sacked their third quarterback, Jim Zorn, for a safety at the end. Naturally, we had beaten up all of their quarterbacks. Just abused them. Five sacks. That's just the way the D was.

It was a good show, and I think it helped get everybody's mind off of the humbling week the head coach had had. Yeah, it had been a humiliating thing, and maybe it just showed I could make mistakes like anybody. Was I perfect? No. But we're

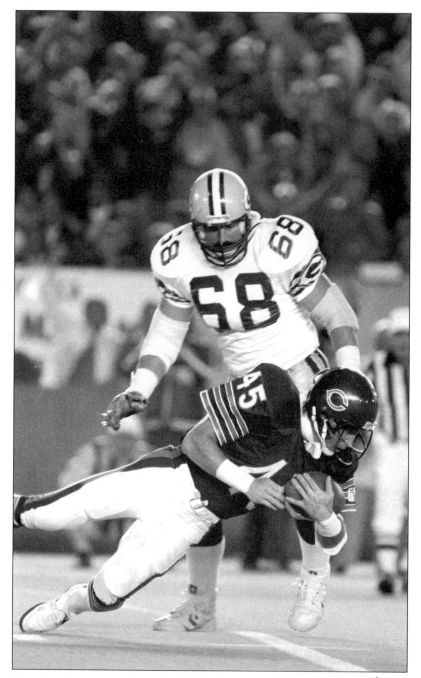

Gary Fencik was a coach on the field for the defense. *Jonathan Daniel/Getty Images*

flying back from a huge win, we're at 35,000 feet for four hours, there's some wine, we have that good feeling you get from doing something well. . . . But in life, we learn and we move on.

Things changed. William Perry was booked to be on David Letterman, and he was getting offers to do ads, T-shirts, posters, endorsements, all kinds of things. I heard somebody was even talking about a toy robot of Fridgie. Maybe they could have called it by the other nickname Hampton gave him, "Mudslide." And pretty soon Buddy started using him on defense, moving Hampton to end and sitting Mike Hartenstine more. I won't say Buddy was surrendering. He would never use that word, never say it. But he backed off a little because he realized Perry deserved to be on the field and that his defensive line needed relief at times.

In fact, with a guy like Perry, the NFL was actually changing, moving to a new place. There were only a couple big guys back when I played, guys like Les Bingaman. But I hardly remember anybody being over 300 or even close to 300. In 1985 America liked this fat stuff. It appealed to the regular guy. It was a novelty. Who would have guessed that in 20 years there would be 300-pounders everywhere in the NFL and people even bigger than Fridge just walking down the streets?

My main concern was still injuries—injuries to Jim McMahon more than anybody else. Keeping him healthy was almost impossible. He practiced like a lineman. He showed little or no regard for his body. I really think he was trying to prove to his teammates that, "Hey, I am the toughest guy out here." I think a lot of offensive players bought into what he was doing. Jesus, he'd do head butts with Van Horne, bad neck, bad back and all! Even the defensive players bought into it. This guy was crazy, in a football way, and they couldn't help but appreciate that.

Whether you liked Jim McMahon or not, he was a tough football player and a good leader by example. He was kind of nuts, but I think ultimately he was respected by everybody on our team. He drove me insane and he pissed me off. I guarantee you he and Hampton didn't get along. But he could lead, because deep down inside all that stuff, he had a brilliant football mind. He had a near photographic memory for downs, situations, blitzes, alignments, weaknesses, all of it. But I think he is wacky, and I think he didn't cultivate it. His different drum beat was he had an authority problem—me, his dad, his head football coach in college, Lavelle Edwards. He was a Catholic and he went to BYU—all Mormons—and I heard BYU never forgot, either. I'll bet he tested that program more than anyone in history. He had his own problems, and he has worked on those throughout his life. And as I said, we all make mistakes. But he was what he was. And we rode it. When we could.

Coming into the week of the second Minnesota game, Jim had a bruised arm, a sprained ankle, and a sore butt cheek that was black and blue and hemorrhaging. Would he be able to play? Who knew?

As it turned out, he did play, and the O-line kept him off his posterior. Wally ran for over 100 yards, and Fridge played for the first time at nose tackle, on first downs, precisely why we drafted him. He got his first sack, too, when he nailed Tommy Kramer on their opening possession. I didn't even use him on offense, because we never had a goal-line situation. See, Buddy? This guy wasn't a wasted draft choice.

We beat the Vikings pretty easily 27-9. We were 8-0 and cooking.

Looking at the old papers, I see that really dumb-ass Dunkel thing. Even a stupid Dunkel can figure stuff out eventually. At

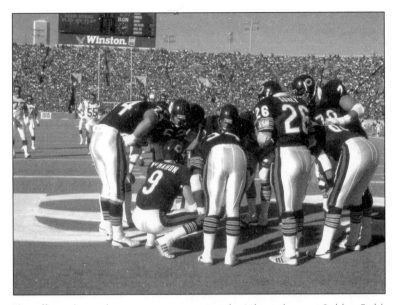

The offense has a long way to go against the Vikings here at Soldier Field. Doesn't matter. The journey has begun. *Photo by Vernon J. Biever*

last we were rated No. 1 in the NFL. Took them long enough to figure it out.

But now it was Packer Week again, and we were going up to Green Bay. This wasn't Soldier Field tailgating. There weren't going to be Bears fans anywhere. There was a lot of mouthiness going on already, especially, it seemed to me, from their side. They were only 3-5, but the Packers-Bears series is like a division within the division. Lose to them, and it diminishes anything else you accomplish.

Like I said, I didn't hate the Packers. When I went up there as a rookie coach in 1982, they had one of the classiest guys I'd ever met in my life at coach, Bart Starr. I had great respect for him, both as a player and a leader. Here it is, my first game, and they put on the Lambeau scoreboard, "THE GREEN BAY

PACKERS WELCOME MIKE DITKA AND THE CHICAGO BEARS." They didn't have to do that. Everybody was saying this is hostile country, but that was just classy.

I wasn't so sure now. Maybe they were still mad about Fridge running over them. Maybe George Cumby represented the little guys who get in the way of a concrete mixer. I don't know, but the Packers came out and were dirtier than dirt. It was disgusting. Just a few minutes into the game this defensive back named Mark Lee hit Payton after Walter was already out of bounds and knocked him into the wall beyond the bench. What the hell was that? They threw Lee out of the game. And it only fired up Walter. The guy had over 100 yards rushing *by halftime.* He had 192 yards for the game, his most in eight years. But this was just chickenshit. I was so angry I could have busted my clipboard into sawdust. Packers players had towels with hit lists on them. They absolutely did.

Some clown named Ken Stills had already hit McMahon late and hard. Then he came flying up from I don't know how far away and creamed Suhey from the blind side three or four seconds after a play was over. Suhey was a tough kid, but he could have been really hurt bad. Stills got a 15-yard penalty, but he should have been thrown out of the game, too. It was the most gutless move I think I've ever seen, because if he'd done it straight, Matt would've kicked his ass from here to next year. And if Stills was told to do it by his coach, his coach is gutless, too.

It was ugly. I might have told my team to retaliate, but I'm not sure if I did. Anyway, they didn't. We just played football. That's all you can do. I think even a lot of Packers fans were embarrassed by the actions of some of their players. Those actions were horrendous. They stunk. It was the ultimate cowardliness that I'd ever seen on a field. It was so contrary to everything the Packers stood for. This might have been the only

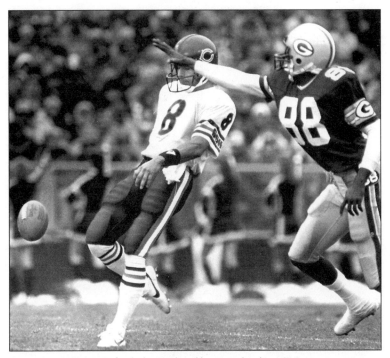

Our punter Maury Buford chipped in, like everybody in '85.
Jonathan Daniel/Getty Images

time there was actual hatred between the teams. And I maintain to this day that it was instigated by one man, their coach. If you can't control your team, then it's your fault. The league didn't fine guys back then like they do now, or that might have got the players' attention, since Forrest Gregg sure didn't. There might have been some of the biggest fines ever given in sports. Walter said after the game he thought Lee was a guy trying to impress his coach. And he probably was.

The reason the Packers were doing all of this was because they weren't good enough to line up against us nose to nose and beat us. In 1983 we were playing the Detroit Lions and they

I was just happy Matt Suhey survived the cheap-shot artists up in Green Bay. Otherwise, he wouldn't have been around to star in the Super Bowl.
Jonathan Daniel/Getty Images

had us basically beaten, and then they faked a field goal and threw a touchdown pass to pile it on. I was hot. I got Dave Duerson, who was a rookie, and told him that on the kickoff I didn't care what happened, I wanted him to knock Lions kicker Eddie Murray on his ass. Maybe some players wouldn't have done it, but Dave did. He knocked the crap out of Murray. Just blasted him. The Detroit coaches were out of their minds, screaming at us, yelling to the refs. It was legal. They're all wearing pads. Just because he's a kicker doesn't mean he can't get hit. But maybe it wasn't right.

Anyway, I was young and madder than they were. But Murray never talked to me again. I used to play in some golf tournaments, and he'd be there and he would just turn the other way.

Detroit's coach back then was Monte Clark, and I know he was a good guy. The problem was mine. It was basically me not knowing what it took to be a mature, solid head coach. We played the Seahawks in 1982 when I was a rookie coach, and they ran a triple reverse on us for big yardage, and the press asked me about it afterward. I said it was a stupid-ass high school play. That was wrong, too. I had no reason to say that. I learned that the other guys are always going to remember what you said. And if you'll notice, after a couple years, I never gave the opponent any more bulletin-board material. I never said a word.

In the Green Bay game, not that I was trying to make a point or anything, but I sent William Perry in for a play just before half. We were down 3-0 at the time, and I knew the Packers thought Fridge was going to steamroll somebody, probably Cumby, all over again. We put William in motion to the right—he looked like a sumo wrestler heading for the ring—and then he slid along the line of scrimmage toward the end zone. The defender had braced for a collision, but Fridge went past him, and McMahon threw him a perfect pass for a four-yard touchdown. Perry caught it with his hands like it was a basketball, his hands reversed from the way football receivers do it, and walked in untouched. Gregg had to be furious. That put us ahead 7-3, and we hung on to win 16-10. I'm not sure, but I think McMahon gave Forrest the finger as he ran off for halftime. Sorry about that.

Some Chicago writer called Perry the "Galloping Roast," and Gary Fencik said what was true: using Perry as a threat was funny, but "he has to be taken seriously." Damn right. I refuse to make it all drudgery. I just don't believe in that. But the fun is effective. Why shouldn't it be? I look at all of these coaches nowadays and you see them in press conferences and, hell, you can't figure out if they won or lost. Does his wife love him or did she just divorce his sorry ass? Mr. Blankface, what's your problem? It's like all of you guys have been cloned. HAVE SOME FUN!

That's why I like this new Atlanta Falcons coach, Jim Mora, Jr. He has fun. I liked his father, too, the old Saints coach. The papers called Fridge the Galloping Roast? At least they didn't say he was the "Stuffed Turkey." I told you how amazing it was to see him on this diet in later years and him working so hard in practice and still not losing weight. Of course, I found out they were bringing pizzas and cases of beer into the dorm late at night, and he'd be wolfing the stuff down—I think he could drink a case of beer no problem—and then he'd be five pounds heavier at weigh-ins the next morning. And he couldn't figure out why his diet wasn't working.

The thing is, sports are a one-time thing. You better do what you can when you can do it. Maybe you can be a doctor for 50 years, or drive a truck that long, but your sports career comes and goes in a hurry. I heard from somebody later in the season that Michael Jordan had broken his foot and had already

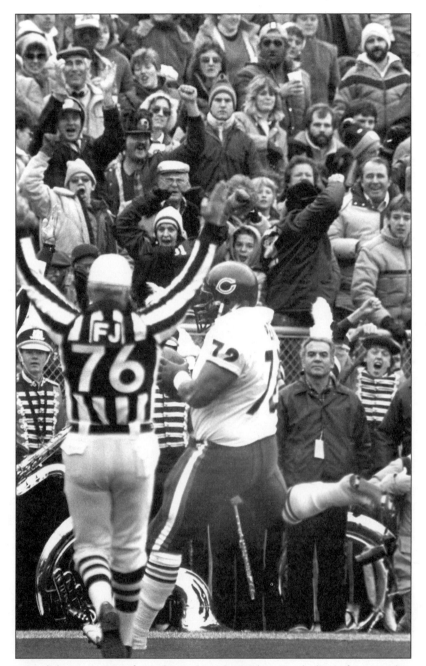

A touchdown reception for Fridge against the Packers. I'm thinking of entering him in the Olympic hurdles next. *Jonathan Daniel/Getty Images*

been out for weeks. And there he was just starting his second year with the Bulls after an unbelievable rookie season. He was probably out for a long time. You never know. That's why this was so important. Right now. This season. This week. This practice. This play.

So far, so good.

We had been forced to come from behind six times, but we were still undefeated. And we were halfway to our goal.

Everybody was a star on the 1985 team, even the offensive line. Wonder if they stole the shades from McMahon's trunk? *Photo by Jean Moss*

No. 34. The best football player I've ever seen.
Photo by Vernon J. Biever

Butthead at rest. It broke my heart to cut veteran kicker Bob Thomas, but kicker Kevin Butler was a great addition to the team. *Photo by Vernon J. Biever*

McMahon tested me, but I knew he could lead the Bears where they'd never been before—if he could stay in one piece. *Photo by Vernon J. Biever*

Dan Hampton's mangled fingers always seemed to find the ball.
Jonathan Daniel/Getty Images

That's me in the two-tone hat with some barking dogs—Otis Wilson and Wilbur Marshall. *Jonathan Daniel/Getty Images*

Who doesn't need a track star like Willie Gault? Pure speed and grace. *Photo by Vernon J. Biever*

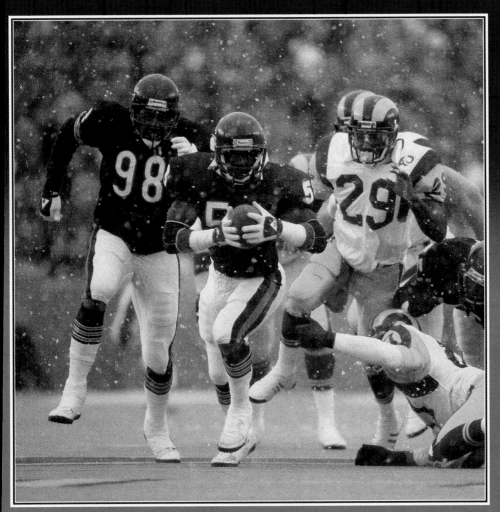

Wilbur Marshall takes a recovered fumble all the way to seal the NFC championship against the Rams. It was a perfect scene—Bears weather, Bears football, Bears dominance. *John Biever/Sports Illustrated*

McMahon could show classic form, if needed. *Michael Zagaris/Getty Images*

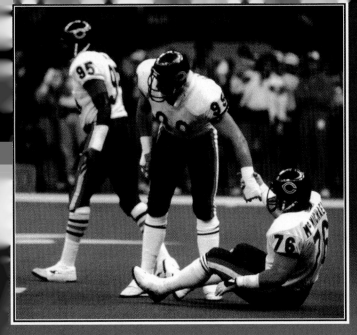

Richard Dent, Hampton, and Steve McMichael—picking each other up in New Orleans.
Photo by Vernon J. Biever

If I could do it again, I'd have Payton score in that Super Bowl. I never meant to let him down. I would do anything for Walter. *Jonathan Daniel/Getty Images*

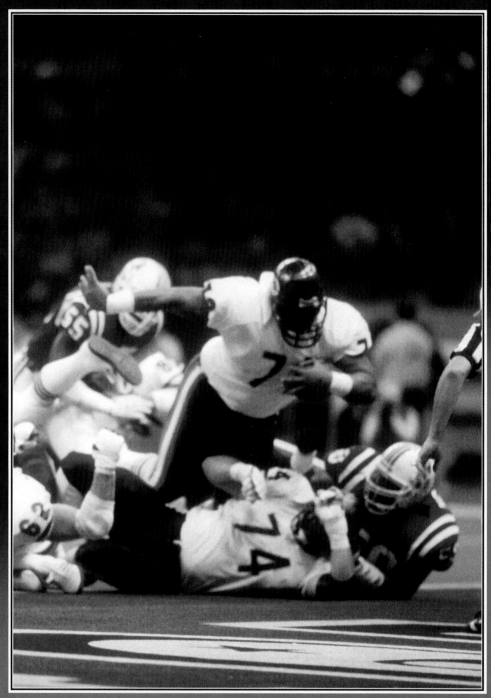
The building didn't collapse when Fridge scored his Super Bowl TD.
Mike Powell/Getty Images

Chapter Ten

Howling Sounds and Defenders from Another Planet

After the Packers game Walter Payton had danced past reporters, saying, reminiscent of the old Jackie Gleason Honeymooners line, "Nine-and-oh, and away we go!"

The Bears were definitely in high gear. Except, of course, for Jim McMahon, who was dealing with leaking tires and busted gaskets. Now his right shoulder was sprained. In practice early in the week, he threw left-handed. Not well, but he threw. But he could barely lift his right arm and had been told by trainer Fred Caito not to use it. Jimmy Mac grinned his twisted grin and said, "I enjoy pain." It was a good marriage, then. But as the days before the Detroit Lions game passed, it became clearer that McMahon was not going to be fit to play, perhaps for a while.

Also thrown into that week was the finding on Thursday in Schaumburg Circuit Court of a guilty verdict for Ditka of driving under the influence after the 49ers game. Ditka was subdued and reasonable in court. His attorney, Don Reuben, complained that Ditka had been handcuffed "and trussed like a chicken." Asked by judge Earl B. Hoffenberg if his client had been abusive toward the arresting officer, Reuben replied, "I suspect anyone would be cantankerous if they were handcuffed."

"You are a well-known public figure," the judge said to Ditka. "You have a great deal of influence over young adults."

The coach nodded, saying he had been speaking to young people about responsible driving for some time. He was sentenced to a year of court supervision, fined $300, and ordered to attend at least 10 hours of driving school. Basically, he needed to do his penance, and steer clear of further arrests, and matters would work out fine.

I still thought I wasn't guilty. I had only been clocked at 63 in a 55-mph zone, and there were cars going past me at 95. Go 55, and you'll get killed. But that was 20 years ago, and I'm not mad at anyone. The judge made his decision, and that's that. It was very embarrassing for me; to the Bears; to Jerry Vainisi, who's my friend; to the players; and to my family. But I didn't lose authority with the team. And I think that is because they realized I was just a regular guy who had made a mistake.

And now I knew that McMahon was definitely out. There wouldn't be any off-the-bench heroics like in the first Vikings game. Steve Fuller had to play, and he hadn't started since that game. He's a good guy, and he handled the way he got yanked, and Jim came in very well.

There was pressure on us now, because we were everybody's target. But what I remember is how windy it was going into that game. It was mid-November, and it was cold and wet, but mostly it was incredibly windy. I watched warmups before the game, and the wind was roaring out of the north like crazy. The flags looked like they were hooked to airplanes. Passes went everywhere. Sid Luckman couldn't have thrown in that wind.

So I decided to run the ball. The first 21 plays I called were runs. Maybe that was overdoing it. Yeah, it was overdoing it. Hell, for the game we ran 55 times! But I was starting to get a little tight, and I didn't want a game like this to slip away because of interceptions or stuff that was almost accidental. I knew this was how I lost the 49ers game in the playoffs last year, by being too conservative, but I didn't want mistakes to be the reason the Lions won. Payton and Suhey both rushed for over 100 yards. I guess inside I knew the Lions weren't that good. They couldn't stop us, and we won 24-3.

The only time I used Fridge on offense, he went in motion again, like that pass play. But Fuller snuck it in from the one for a touchdown. Perry was definitely a big deal, though. On Monday he went to New York to be on Letterman. He had his front tooth out, as always, but he had a coat and tie and sweater vest on, and he looked nice. Letterman asked him if it was true he had once drunk 48 beers after a Clemson victory over North Carolina. Fridge nodded and said, "It was a big game."

The thing is a team consists of a lot of different people. Steve McMichael and Mike Singletary were both from Texas, but after that they were about as different as two people could be. McMichael was like a Harley-Davidson biker. Singletary was like a minister. I think he might have *been* a minister, might have actually had ministry papers. I don't think they ever had a conversation that lasted more than seven seconds. So what? They respected each other. And they both had huge hearts.

We didn't have the NFL combine back in those days, thank God, because neither of them would have impressed anybody at an idiotic meat market like that. Singletary, I mean, he's in the Hall of Fame. He had a great study and work ethic, and he was intelligent. And he had discipline. But he was short and he wore glasses, and how do you think he would have rated in the computers? Those combines are unadulterated bullshit. You go to Indianapolis and watch somebody run 40s and lift weights and jump around, and you think you can tell me he's going to be a great football player? IQ tests are nothing. How many times do they hand you pencils out on the field?

When I came out of college, it was even more primitive. In my rookie training camp Halas said he wanted me to run a 40.

I said, "Why?"

He said, "I just want you to run it."

So I did. And I ran a 4.7 on grass, maybe like a 4.73, which surprised me. That's pretty good. Of course, it was before I dislocated my foot. But I knew I could run. I knew it my whole life, from when I was a kid and I ran everywhere. That's what you do. There were guys who were fast as hell, but I watched Walter Payton run, and I watched Barry Sanders run, and they weren't all that fast. But I never saw people catching them from behind.

There were true sprinters like Bob Hayes and my one-time roommate Johnny Morris, who had some short indoor record

Samurai had only one speed, only one desire. Nobody was going to deny him.
Photo by Vernon J. Biever

like the 50-yard dash or something. But I saw Willie Galimore beat him by five yards in a 40. Willie, man, he could fly. And so could his buddy, Johnny Farrington. They were as exciting as it gets. They were Bears teammates of mine back in the early days. Galimore was a back out of Florida A&M, and he ran for 181 yards in a game my second year. Farrington, whose nickname was Bo, was a wide receiver from Prairie View, and he still holds the Bears' longest reception record, 98 yards.

They were on our 1963 championship team, and we should have had a great team in 1964. But one night at preseason training camp down in Rensselaer, Indiana, in August 1964, Willie and Bo went to a country club bar to watch the Olympics on TV and maybe have a beer or two. It was an off-day and they were coming back and they were on this twisting highway that led to camp. The mowers had just cut the grass, and I think they took down some signs that pointed out the curves. Willie was driving and he went off the road and then swerved to get back on, and one of the wheels evidently collapsed and the car rolled. It was a Volkswagen with the top open, and Willie flew out the roof and was killed, and then the car rolled over and broke Johnny's neck and killed him.

I was 24 years old, and the next morning I went down to the morgue with my teammates Rick Casares and Bill George, and I looked at the bodies on the slab. There was not one mark on Willie, not one mark. And Farrington had a cut on his face.

It was devastating to me. It was devastating to the team. We should have been really good in 1964, but we went 5-9, and it was like our soul had been cut out. I know we're all going to die. That's why you have to try hard when you've got your chance, and it's why you shouldn't let the trivial things make you crazy. Way back, I was ridiculous. Are you kidding me? It got to the point where it was beyond stupidity, with my anger and all. Like with Harbaugh on the sideline, even then I was 500 times wrong, but I was so pissed off about that audible I wanted to kill him. Same with Avellini. Why? Why couldn't I just pat him on the back and say, "Don't do it again"?

Maybe it came from just wanting to win so bad. Back when I was in Little League in Aliquippa, I'd be pitching, and a teammate would make an error, and I'd get so mad I'd tell the manager I wanted to play that position and to bring in another pitcher. I was nuts. But I just think that winning is important. Because if you line up in life and you accept defeat, then you will be defeated. And you'll get what you were ready for. When you quit, you're defeated. Right there. That's the equation. If you keep fighting, you've got a chance.

Look, you can't say you're going to be the greatest in everything. Take singing, for instance. You want to sing like Sinatra? We have a singer here at the bar who is very good, John Vincent, who sounds a hell of a lot like Frank. But in fourth grade the nun told me, "Michael, it sounds like you're howling. Do NOT sing." So I wasn't going anywhere with my voice. I will not be singing here at my cigar bar, for instance.

Do we pick the things we're good at, or do they pick us? I'm not sure it matters. When I was a kid, I was a pretty good baseball player. I had a big strike zone, but if I got hold of it, it went. I played at Pitt, and one game we played against Kent State, and they had a pitcher who ended up with the Yankees. He put one down the middle and, man, I blasted it way over the center field wall. It was big time. Tommy Lasorda scouted me, and years later he said, "You had a big strike zone, but I watched you hit one way over the fence."

I had a chance to sign a minor league contract. But I wanted to go to college and get an education, even though I had no idea what that really meant or what it would be in. My high school coach said, "You should study dentistry. You can be a dentist

I believe in respecting the game, the foe, and the country. Even if I can't sing on key. *Jonathan Daniel/Getty Images*

and come back here and make great money." Sounded good to
me.

So you get into the what-ifs. What if I had gone to Pitt and
blown out my knee, and that was it for sports? I guess I would
have come back to Aliquippa and worked in the steel mill. The
dentistry thing wouldn't have happened. I mean, think of Dr.
Ditka. Me looking in people's mouths? I think I'd rather knock
teeth out than put them in. But you don't know. Maybe I
wouldn't have quit school; maybe I would have become that
dentist. And a good one. A nice, sweet dentist. The point is, my
life wouldn't have ended. What would have happened if I'd
gotten hurt? I never really have thought about it. None of that
"Why me, not him?" stuff. I played with a lot of guys from all
over the state of Pennsylvania, tough kids, and they hurt a knee
or whatever and were never the same. It's a risk, but you don't
think about it. Back then, you hurt your knee, it was like
butchery—they put your leg in a huge cast, and your career
could be finished.

At Pitt we came in with a hardnosed freshman class, and I
remember in one scrimmage we kicked the shit out of the
varsity. Because we wanted it bad. There's fate involved in life,
but I don't think the key to life is chance. It's when you realize
what an opportunity you have, and you snatch it. I got a chance
to play football and a chance to coach it, and that was enough
for me. I made up my mind a long time ago that eventually I
would coach the Chicago Bears. I didn't know how it would
happen. There was a lot of dumb stuff along the way. I had to
grow up. I left Chicago on bad terms with Mr. Halas. And then
at the end, in 1992, I was terminated by the powers that be.
That was 100 percent jealousy. One McCaskey at the top was
never thrilled with me, and now he wanted everything for
himself. So it goes.

Me and my old pal, Cowboys assistant coach Ernie Stautner. I had mixed feelings about destroying Dallas. *Jonathan Daniel/Getty Images*

But what I could always come back to was this: I'd been drafted by the man who started the NFL. And the man who started it had asked me to coach. That's a pretty close connection to the roots of football. Not like being the Pope, but it was pretty good.

Now we had the Dallas Cowboys coming up. Halas may have given me more opportunities than anyone else, but nobody flat-out helped me more than Cowboys coach Tom Landry. It was almost like we were going from Forrest Gregg, who was Darth Vader, to Moses.

Everybody needs help in life. When you come to the Y in the road, you have to take one way or the other. When I came to the Y, Coach Landry was standing there, and he said, "Come this way." And I went that way, and that's basically that. He believed I could be a coach. I know he was worried that if I couldn't control myself, how could I control others? But he let me work on that.

The main thing he told me when I finally got the Bears job was, "Whether you succeed or not, do it your way. Don't ever leave yourself open to doing it somebody else's way, and then blame them if you fail." That was wonderful advice, because at the beginning I did listen to everybody. Who doesn't? Tom was more important to me than anyone in a way, even more than my dad. I had a great high school coach. And Coach Halas was my coach as a football player. But Tom was my coach as a *coach*.

I basically brought his offense to the Bears. I changed a few things, but I even numbered the holes the way he did, which was very unusual. We had the odd numbers—1, 3, 5, 7, 9—to the right, and the even—2, 4, 6, 8—to the left. Everybody in football does it the opposite way, But not in Dallas. I think Tom did it that way because he was looking at it from the defensive standpoint, seeing it from their eyes. I did it his way. I couldn't change it.

I know people said we were about as different as two people could be, him so stoic and calm, and me all keyed-up. But I looked up to him. And I think he saw something in me he respected and appreciated, and maybe he even was a little like me. He knew, no matter what, how much I cared about the game and doing things well. I'd been his player and then his assistant, and now that I was an NFL head coach, we still talked all the time. I needed his advice on so many things. I could call, and he would always be there for me. He was my biggest booster.

So now we have to play his team, the Cowboys, "America's Team," down in Dallas. And they're pretty good, as they always were under Tom. They're 7-3 and in first place in the NFC East. This was another big test for us. We got past the Redskins and the 49ers and the Packers, twice. And we had the undefeated streak. But Dallas is Dallas. They beat us last year, the only time we'd played them since I started coaching the Bears. We were only favored by a point.

McMahon was definitely out; his shoulder tendinitis wasn't improving, so Fuller was my guy again. Good old Steve. I loved him to death. But was he up to this? And I didn't know how I felt for sure about this contest. I was the pupil going against the teacher. I had a lot of emotions going around. Believe me, I was pretty chewed up inside.

And then we played. And we annihilated Dallas. Buddy's philosophy was simple: "Take the sum-bitch away from them in a hurry." Meaning the ball. Our defense mutilated the Cowboys. It became like a snowball going downhill. Those poor Dallas quarterbacks didn't know whether to shit or go blind. I can still see their backup quarterback Gary Hogeboom, when he was already on his way to the turf and Singletary hit him so hard before he could reach the ground that I thought Mike had killed him.

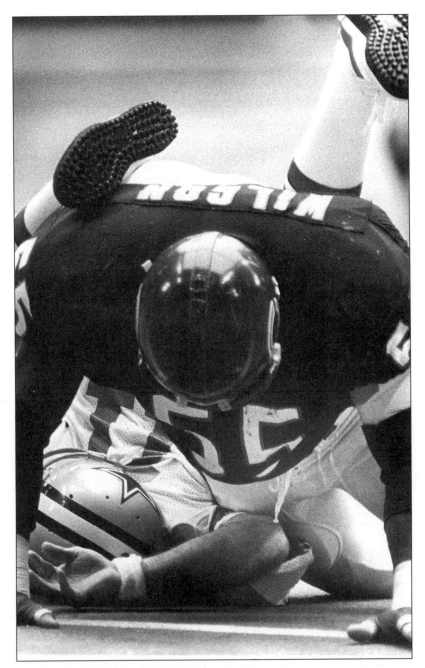

Otis looks down to see if Dallas QB Danny White is alive or Memorex.
Jonathan Daniel/Getty Images

The offense was solid. We gained almost 400 yards, and Payton had another 100-yard day. But the defense shut everything down. Richard Dent caught a pass tipped by Hampton at the goal line and ran it in for a touchdown. Cornerback Mike Richardson ran an interception back for a score. Les Frazier had a long interception return. Otis Wilson knocked their starting quarterback, Danny White, out of the game. Twice. Jeez, I started to feel sorry for White, down on the turf, his helmet off, half-conscious. Our defense was crazy, like attack dogs, and they started barking. "Woof! Woof!"

Somewhere in the third quarter I said to Buddy, "Can you slow these guys down?"

And he said, "Mike, I can't."

Our defense was gone. On another planet.

We won 44-0 with a backup quarterback. It was the worst loss for Dallas, ever. By the end Texas Stadium was silent, except for all of the Bears fans, who were barking and singing.

I felt good, but I also felt bad. Here we were, doing what we could only dream about doing. And yet it was the worst thing, too. We had our picture taken before the game, Coach Landry and me, our arms around each other. This was the guy I'd learned everything from. He was a good racquetball player, and when I was coaching under him, he and I and Dan Reeves and Ernie Stautner and a bunch of guys would play after practice. We had fun, and then he'd say, "Go home. Be with your families. If we can't get our work done during the day, something's wrong." He never asked the assistants to stay real late. He taught me that sometimes you overthink things, you try to change game plans so much that you're just messing with something that isn't broken. There was probably nothing he was prouder of than when Dan Reeves and I both became head coaches after studying under him.

But 44-0?

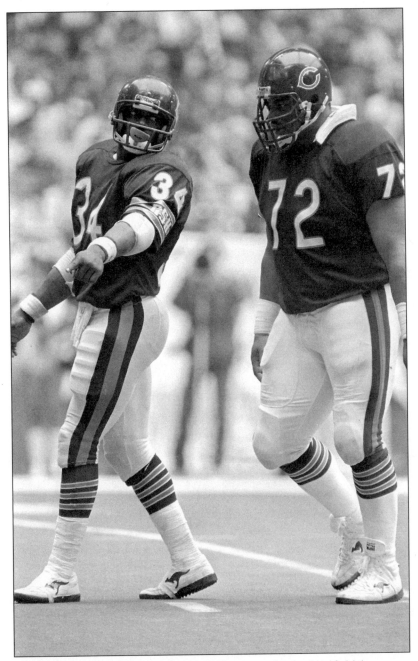

Payton tells running mate Perry where to line up. Maybe this backfield thing is out of control. *Jonathan Daniel/Getty Images*

In life there are conflicts like that. It hurt. But I remember just a week before I'd been watching *Monday Night Football* and Redskins quarterback Joe Theismann got hit by Lawrence Taylor, and his leg broke in half. Compound fracture. They caught it on tape. And it made me sick.

But that was life. Life went on.

And now I wanted to go without a loss, ever.

Chapter Eleven

Traveling South, Near-Blows with Buddy, Monday Night Hell

The Bears horse-whipped the lowly Atlanta Falcons 36-0 the next week. It was more of the same. More defense. More Payton. More McMahon still out with injuries—mainly that bad shoulder. Indeed, rumors from Halas Hall were that McMahon might be done for the season. The Fridge got himself an airborne one-yard touchdown dive in the blowout, a move he said he copied after further studying Payton's leaping heroics. According to the Sun-Times, Perry's self-launch to paydirt "alarmed both air traffic controllers and earthquake monitors."

Ditka was amused and a little awestricken himself by the carnage. "They must have felt like it was Sherman's army marching through them," he said of the Atlantans. Even third-string Bears quarterback Mike Tomczak got some quality minutes in the rout.

The Bears were playing at a level never seen in the NFL. The "46" defense looked like a single wave of attackers storming a straw hut. Mike Singletary was outraged when he learned Atlanta running back Gerald Riggs had gained 100 yards, the first 100-yard game given up by the defense since the opener against Tampa Bay, when James Wilder got 166. "You have to understand Mike," Ditka said. "And his pride."

Now the obvious challenge for the Bears was to go without a loss. Standing in the way of the 12-0 team was this week's opponent, the Miami Dolphins. The game was to be at the Orange Bowl, the Dolphins' home field, where coach Don Shula and his young genius quarterback Dan Marino ruled. Indeed, the Dolphins had won 17 of their last 18 games in the always-jammed, old-fashioned, humid and palm tree-dotted arena. It was a fitting matchup, because it was Shula's 1972 Dolphins who were the only team in NFL history to go undefeated, including winning the Super Bowl. That 1972 team had a curious parallel to the Bears' 1985 team in that in the previous season the Dolphins had marched all of the way to the Super Bowl, only to lose. Those 1971 Dolphins had lost 24-3 to the Dallas Cowboys, who featured a tight end named Mike Ditka.

"We got beat, and we didn't like it," then-Miami quarterback Bob Griese said later. "So really our season started with a loss the year before." Same with the Bears. Their 23-0 spanking in the 1984 NFC championship game had festered badly. At the end of the Bears' 44-0 demolition of the Cowboys two weeks earlier, inflamed and single-minded middle-linebacker/preacher Mike Singletary had turned to the Texas crowd and screamed, "Don't leave! I want witnesses!"

Going undefeated in the NFL wasn't just hard. It was a transcendent goal; maybe, with the extended schedule, impossible. The 1972 Dolphins had finished 17-0. Prior to Super Bowl play, NFL teams only played a maximum of 13 games, final game included. Now the Bears would have to go 19-0—16 regular-season games and three playoff games—to achieve perfection. That didn't stop Bears analysts from crowing. A headline above Sun-Times *football writer Kevin Lamb's column said, "If Stats Don't Lie, It's Bears By 40."*

Stats weren't going to mean much in this face-off on national TV, again an ABC Monday Night *spectacular. This would be about intangibles, luck, bounces. The Bears were well on their way to being the first team since those undefeated 1972 Dolphins to lead the NFL in points scored and fewest points allowed. They were ahead of everyone by 40 offensively and 45 defensively. In the last four games they had outscored their opponents 120-13. The average score of their last three games—all quarterbacked by Steve Fuller— was a ridiculous, 35-1. Still...*

The contest would be the highest rated for Monday Night Football, *ever. Even to this day. Everybody tuned in to see the battle, to see these barking dogs, this high wire act, this invading horde, and the obstacle in front of them.*

McMahon is still hurt, but I'm used to it now. He makes a crack about how he needs to play so he can make some money on his incentives, so he can pay all the fines I've laid on him. I don't know about that. If I fined anybody that year, it was minimal. Really minimal. I had rules, but they weren't much. I probably had a double standard for some guys. But I don't remember fining many guys that year. I hated to take their money. I used to play the game, and I remembered what it was like when the Old Man fined me. Goddamn, that bothered me! In retrospect, yeah, I deserved it. But it pissed me off.

In a sense, there's no question I was too compassionate toward the players. Not the coaches, maybe . . . but the players. I know later on I kept guys too long, after they were done. But I couldn't help it. I always remembered being a player, how your life was in the hands of the coach.

We're traveling to Miami and not much of this is on my mind, because all I'm thinking of is what a great coach Don Shula is and what a great passer Marino is. Still, I knew we had a team that was incredible.

We get to the Orange Bowl, and the crowd is at a fever pitch. That's fine. Cops have German Shepherds on leashes. We're used to noise and craziness by now. It was humid but not hot, because this is already the beginning of December. Somebody has told me we've lost our last eight *Monday Night* games when we're on the road. Yeah? Screw 'em. Screw those statistics, all of it. This isn't a pinball game. This is football.

But something is wrong with this night. The Dolphins are having Marino roll away from Dent, which is smart, but we can't get to him with the other guys. They're using little wide receiver Nat Moore like a tight end, putting him the slot and putting him in motion. We've seen three-receiver sets, but this has three wideouts and no true tight end. So we have to cover Moore with a linebacker like Wilbur Marshall or, after a while, we moved Fencik up in man-to-man, but he's more of a deep safety, and that's not a good matchup, either.

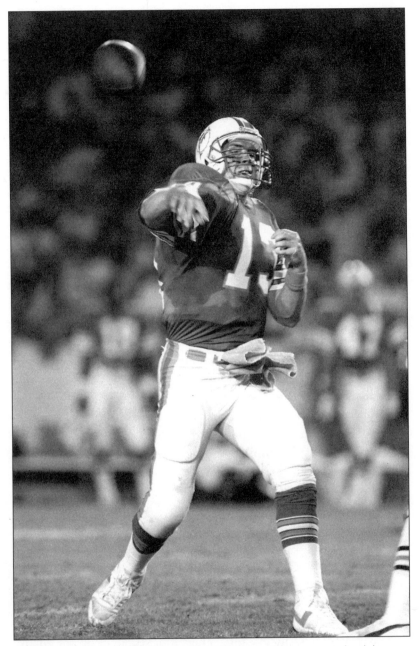

Dan Marino shot bullets in our undefeated season. What a quarterback he was. But I'll still maintain that our defense could have stopped him if Buddy had adjusted. *Jonathan Daniel/Getty Images*

Now, Dent is an impact player. He should be in the Hall of Fame, no question about it. He was the 203rd player taken in the 1983 draft out of dinky Tennessee State, and he was skinny and raw and hadn't played against anybody. But he worked his ass off, bulked up, used his athleticism. I kidded him, calling him Robert, but that was just because he wanted more money, more publicity, and I was messing with him. But he was the real deal, a great pass-rushing defensive end.

Thing was, in this game Marino stayed away from him. Marino did his half-rollouts to stay away, and he had that quick release. A quick-draw gunslinger's gun. The problem is, Dent can't do anything, because he's got to go 15 yards or more to get to Marino, and we're asking our linebackers, guys who are used to going straight ahead, to drop back in coverage. We should have gone to a nickel. Five defensive backs. They're running what is essentially a third down-and-long formation a whole lot of the time. They hadn't shown that before. Not throughout an entire game. And we didn't adjust. Sure, it was more complicated than that, but that was at the root of it.

Steve Fuller was doing what he could on offense. He never worried about his limitations, he never worried about being a star, about notoriety, none of it. He was a true team player, and he had confidence, because he'd had early success with the Kansas City Chiefs. He planned and prepared like nobody else. He was very smart—he was a Rhodes Scholar candidate at Clemson—and he's made a great success in real estate down in South Carolina since his football career ended. I never looked at him as just a backup, but, still, it was McMahon, the rebel grenade, who could do the genius things. And he was on the bench.

Miami got lucky, too. They blocked a punt by Maury Buford and recovered it at our six. They even had a horseshit pass that Hampton deflected, and it should have been

Mac was fragile. Where would we have been without dependable backup Steve Fuller? *Photo by Vernon J. Biever*

intercepted, but it went way up in the air, and damned if their toothpick wideout Mark Clayton didn't catch it for a long score. But that wasn't what pissed me off.

No, I was mad at Buddy. Look, what we're doing on defense isn't working. So let's adapt! Wilbur Marshall is one of the best athletes I've seen, but don't ask him to cover wide receivers 30 yards downfield. We should have gone to a straight nickel. Rush four linemen, use two linebackers and have the five DBs cover. Maybe the problem was who do you take out? It might have hurt somebody's ego. Maybe Buddy's. Otis Wilson is a good linebacker, but why didn't we put Reggie Phillips in there in the nickel? If you're not flexible to make adjustments, to change what's not working, you'll never win. The "46" had been ungodly up until this game. But we needed to fine-tune it. Right now! You have to give your players the best chance to win. You can't handicap them. If the tanks are getting blown up, come in with the Air Force. That's all I was saying.

So we come in at halftime, down 31-10. We've given up more points in two quarters than we had in the last six *entire games!* Goddamn, I was furious. Later, people would say I was doing too much off-field stuff, commercials and TV shows and what have you, that I wasn't paying attention to the store. That was bull. My mind was always on the goal.

I go up to Buddy and I start screaming at him. "*What are you doing out there? We have to run the nickel! Let's blitz the shit out of them!*" He yells back at me, and now we've got a pissing match. We're pushing and yelling, and the players are there, and it's not a good thing. It's pretty ugly. Players separate us, and we move apart. I try to calm down. Football is a tense game. I've seen two assistants go at it. But not a head coach and a coordinator. All I'm trying to get across is that you don't let your men get beat just because you won't combat what the other side is doing. I'll go to my grave believing that.

I think Buddy and I resolved the conflict before the half ended. And I think I apologized to him after the game. At any rate, Fuller got hurt in the fourth quarter, so I put McMahon in the game, hoping that maybe he could do stuff just like in that first Minnesota game. But it wasn't there. He had no magic under his hat. He got sacked a couple times and threw an interception. We lost 38-24, and it stunk.

The only good thing that happened was I kept Walter in at the end, handing him the ball so he could get 100 yards. He got 121, his eighth-straight 100-yard game, an NFL record. I wanted him to beat that *Monday Night* TV guy, O.J. Simpson, who had been tied with him at seven. Simpson was always

McMahon with his pads off—hurt again. Amazing how young he looks without sunglasses on. *Jonathan Daniel/Getty Images*

second-guessing us. So now he could second-guess Payton's record.

They told me Fridge's new McDonald's ad had debuted at halftime of the *Monday Night* game. Swell.

Nobody is invincible. And nobody that season was undefeated. Not even us, the mighty Bears.

We had to regroup.

Chapter Twelve

We Can Do Damn Near Everything, but Maybe We Can't Dance

The Indianapolis Colts didn't stand a chance. They were the Bears' next opponent, at Soldier Field, and they weren't a very good team. And the Bears were seething. The final score was 17-10 Bears, but it wasn't that close. Chicago had been leading 17-3, until the Colts scored on a 61-yard pass late in the fourth quarter. Other than that play, the Colts gained only 24 yards and made one first down in the second half. Walter Payton rushed for his ninth-straight 100-yard game, extending his NFL record. And praise be! Jim McMahon played the entire game.

Next up were the New York Jets, a 10-4 team that featured long-haired and flakey defensive end Mark Gastineau, known for sacking quarterbacks and doing a spastic celebratory dance afterward. Ditka had called the Indianapolis win "ugly," and the game against the Jets was no beauty, either. It was close until Kevin Butler made his third and fourth field goals of the game in the last four minutes. The Bears won 19-6. Everything seemed tainted since the Miami loss, but still, the fact was there: the Bears were a 14-1 team.

There were so many great players on that 1985 team, and I sometimes wish I could just tell the world how much they meant to me. Take Butthead. Kevin Butler was like one of the guys. You may say, so what? But kickers are often very unusual people. They're guys who are hard to have conversations with. If you're not careful, they'll start crying or calling for their mother. That's if you can even understand what in the hell they're saying, because they're usually from Austria or somewhere. But Butler was born in Savannah, Georgia, and he went out with the guys and partied and was a football player, the real deal. I liked him. Of course, maybe I wouldn't have liked him so much if he couldn't kick straight. But just in that Jets game he had four field goals. Not real long ones, but needed ones. And he was automatic. Twelve points. Not bad.

William Perry was settling in, doing whatever we asked of him. People might have thought I was all over the map, using this kid like I was. But in the Jets game he picked up a fumble and ran with it seven yards. He may have looked like a barrel rolling across the floor, but he was moving pretty good, in my opinion. I'd already talked to the press about wanting him to run for a touchdown, catch a touchdown pass, and—here was the big one—throw a TD pass. It was fun, but here are two things. One, by doing that it made the other team *have* to prepare for him and maybe forget about what was really important. And two, I could have done the same thing with 10 other guys, but it wouldn't have worked. It worked with William because he was a good enough athlete and a good enough person to handle it. By the end of the season if you said "Refrigerator," people didn't think of a place to put food. They thought of a huge guy who ate food. That's how famous he was.

You think I was eccentric? You think I was intense? Hell, I remember coming back from a loss up in Minnesota when I was a rookie. Coach Halas got on the intercom at the front of the airplane and said, "You're nothing but a bunch of cunts!" I think Michael McCaskey, his own grandson and president of the team, once said I was a lot calmer than Halas.

I suppose I was a product of where I grew up and how I grew up. My dad was old school, absolutely. He was a former Marine. He never went to battle, but he was a Marine. He worked on a railroad that serviced J & L Steel in Aliquippa, which is one of the mill towns up the Ohio River from Pittsburgh. My dad was a car repair man, a welder. A burner is what we called them. His dad was a burner, too, did the same thing.

Dad would come home, and his clothes always had holes in them from the sparks. He had burn marks on his hands and arms, but that's what he did. He was self-taught. I think he went to the seventh grade, at most. But he could do any crossword puzzle I've ever seen. He had a great vocabulary, and with that limited education he became president of his union. Although he defended the workers, he wouldn't defend somebody who wouldn't work. You slept on the job? I got news for you. Pop Ditka was on your ass.

We are Ukranian. My father was born here, but his parents came over from the old country. People called us Polacks, mostly, or Hunkies. I don't know why they couldn't come up with Ukies. We weren't a close family, and it was because my dad was tough. He was tough with my mom. And he was tough with me. He got on me hard, but he didn't go after the other kids. I was the oldest, and I had two brothers and a sister. I was talking to my sister the other day, and I said, "Dad never touched you, did he?"

And she said, "One time when I was a sophomore or junior in high school I said something to him, and he slapped me."

I said, "I never thought he slapped anyone but me."

I know he never touched the other two boys. But he was rough with me and my mom. When you see that as a kid, it bothers you. But then in retrospect you understand that he was raised like that, and that's what he knew. I blamed him for a lot. I didn't like him, basically, until I went off to college and lived away from home. All of my buddies got to do stuff, but I could never be out past nine o'clock until high school. There was a reason why he did it, but I didn't understand his motives until the end: he didn't want me working in the mill. He wanted me to get an education. We kids were going to have a better life than he did.

It took a long time for that to sink in, to explain things, but the more I understood, the better it got. At the end we used to talk a lot, and we had a great relationship even though it was from a distance. It's like that song, "Cat's in the Cradle," by

Harry Chapin. When I had time for him, he had no time for me. When he had time for me, I had no time for him. That's the sadness of getting old with your kids. You can't go back and undo things. But, really, we went from being strangers to being friends by the end.

He died six years ago, at 80, while I was coaching in New Orleans. He had hardening of the arteries and he was a four packs of Lucky Strikes a day guy from the time he was 12 until he quit cold turkey at age 59. Twenty-one years without a smoke, which was pretty good. And he used to go crazy when Diana would light up a cigarette in front of him. He'd shake his head and say, "I'd give anything to have one of those!"

I was the first born, and probably he was hardest on me for two reasons: because I was the oldest and because I deserved it more than the other ones. I had a knack for getting into stupid trouble. Nothing malicious. But if there was something stupid to do, I'd be one of the guys doing it, and I'd always end up getting blamed. I'll give you an example.

One time me and my buddies went to the library during the holidays just to mess around. They had a Christmas tree up, and we stole a couple of ornaments. Why, I don't know. We were dumb-ass kids. So we have these little glass ornaments, those colored balls, and we're running down the street playing catch with them, throwing them back and forth. You know how light they are, and the wind is blowing. So I throw one and the wind catches it and it hits a kid right above his eye. I hit him pretty good. The glass shatters, and he's cut, and there's blood pouring down his face, and he freaks out. He has to get about six stitches.

Me, I have to go to school and tell the nun what happened, and she beats the shit out of me with a ruler. Then I have to go home and tell Dad, and he beats the shit out of me. That's the way it was. I got my ass beat a lot. Now the nuns, maybe they were mean. But I think it was their job to teach you discipline and order, and they didn't allow any messing around. The ones I had, anyway.

Did beating me make me change as a person? No. But it taught me to fear doing something wrong. If you're afraid to do something wrong, you'll avoid it because you don't want your ass whupped. Funny thing is, as a coach I don't believe in it. I know the nuns did, and my dad did, but I don't. I believe that if you're fair with people, you're up front with them, you talk to them, it's better than force. Still, the only way they deterred me from doing even stupider things as a kid was by punishment.

When I went nuts on teammates or players, it was only because winning was so important to me. I got on some guys pretty bad at Pitt, for instance, and I'm not proud of that. But I really couldn't think of another way. I couldn't do it Landry's way. Of course, I didn't know Landry back then. Even Lombardi couldn't have been like Landry. Lombardi was Lombardi. I was myself.

The world can judge you how it wants. I remember we went to London in the summer of 1986. We were playing an exhibition game against the Cowboys at Wembley Stadium for all these ga-ga Englishmen, and we are the rage of the island. This was the NFL's big push into Europe, going global. People had T-shirts with the Fridge on them, No. 72, running with the football. They'd sprint right past Walter Payton to get to Perry. Everybody was famous, though. Willie Gault had stuff going on, and Matt Suhey visited the stock exchange, and, yes, Walter was very important. But he wasn't literally huge, like Perry. The cover of *Sports Illustrated* even showed Fridge with the Cowboys' "Too Tall" Jones standing next to one of the Queen's Royal Guardsmen. I said in a press conference, "I have the best running back in the history of the game, and all you want to know about is a lineman!"

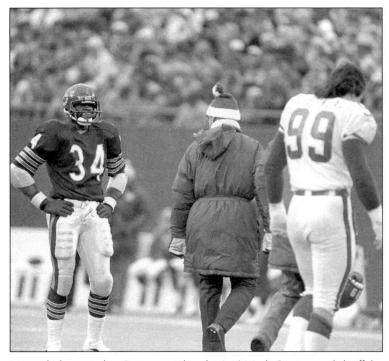

No sack dance today. Payton watches the Jets' Mark Gastineau slink off the field. *Jonathan Daniel/Getty Images*

So anyway, back to 1985. Around the time of our Jets game, Gastineau was getting all of the pub. That didn't bother me. He was a good player, but the New York media made him a lot better than he was. I mean, he couldn't carry Dent's or Hampton's jock strap. He's got a sack dance? Why would you want to do that if you're good and you know it? What does waving your arms around have to do with anything? *Look at me, I'm great!* Prove it by playing.

People said I was doing too many off-field things? My team was? If you still play hard on Sunday, which is when the games are played, that's all that matters. If the players can make a few bucks off the field, good. As for me, I was fully dedicated. To the critics, I said screw you. Besides, I wasn't doing that much, mostly just the TV show with Johnny.

We had one more regular-season game to go, against the Lions, who were an average team. It was there in Detroit, in their stupid dome, but if we played our game and never made mistakes like in the Miami game, we couldn't be beat. Before that game the Pro Bowl teams were announced, and we had eight guys make the roster—Payton, Hampton, Dent, Covert, Hilgenberg, Singletary, Wilson, and even Dave Duerson, who was shocked as shit. They all deserved it. But so did Fencik and Van Horne and Marshall and about five other guys.

Some of the hoopla came from another thing, though. A bunch of the guys, 10 of them, including Payton, Fridge, Fuller, and McMahon, had used one of their off-days to make some kind of rap video. It was Willie Gault's idea, I think, along with some producer. Willie had asked me to be in it, but I'd taken a pass. Dancing? Singing? Are you kidding? You can laugh, because I've done a lot of nutty stuff, such as wear a tuxedo in a "wedding portrait" with my "bride," Ricky Williams. But I didn't give a crap about this thing. Plus, I remembered what that nun had said. I didn't even know what it was about, but real soon I see these giant ads and it's called "The Super Bowl Shuffle"!

My God, we have another regular-season game to play and then we'll have to win two more games in the playoffs just to go to the Super Bowl. Talk about jumping the gun. But hey, I admired the guys' confidence, if that's what it was. People already didn't like us. Like I seemed to be saying more and more: screw 'em.

So we go to Detroit and we win our finale 37-17. Dennis Gentry—little Pinkie—runs a kickoff back for a touchdown, the first against the Lions in five years. And Wilbur Marshall

I hope that animal had a good life. *Photo by Vernon J. Biever*

hits quarterback Joe Ferguson so hard right under the chin that you can see Ferguson is unconscious even before he hits the turf. When Wilbur got fined later by the league, I thought it was bullcrap. I mean, the refs hadn't even called a penalty.

It was an odd game. Even though we won pretty easily, the game bothered me. It was blah. I was certain a good team would beat us, maybe embarrass us. Well, I wasn't certain of that, but I feared it. I couldn't get the Dolphins game out of my mind. William Perry even picked up a fumble and ran until somebody jumped on him. But it didn't matter.

The locker room was very quiet. Everybody knew we had only one goal now that we couldn't go undefeated. And this little win had nothing to do with it. "Maybe we shouldn't do too many Super Bowl Shuffles," I said to the media. I didn't mean that. But I didn't want this thing to get away from us. I was tense and cranky.

We would have home-field advantage all through the playoffs, and we were going to start off against the winner of the 49ers-Giants wildcard game. We had two weeks to kill.

We needed to get shuffling.

Chapter Thirteen

Headband Craziness, A Yuppie Who Likes to Hurt People, the Elephant in the Snow

As the New York Giants wildcard game against the defending
Super Bowl champion San Francisco 49ers was ending, fans at the
Meadowlands in East Rutherford, New Jersey, began chanting, "We
want the Bears! We want the Bears!" The Giants had been
impressive in smacking the 49ers 17-3. But the fact that so many
of the 76,000 howling fans actually wanted a piece of the 15-1
Bears showed a certain audacity that could only come from the
safety of a bleacher seat and a throat warmed by a flask of booze.
   The Bears had gone to the Atlanta Falcons training camp in
Suwanee, Georgia, to practice for the first round.
   Ditka had wanted to set up camp at the University of Illinois
in Champaign, but the plastic bubble that was needed to cover the
field couldn't be erected in time. No matter. It was just geography.
The Bears hadn't changed from what they were. They may have lost
to the Dolphins and had internal squabbling that was
embarrassing and unprofessional, but they hadn't died. They had
been nicked, frustrated, lowered half a notch, and they were angry.
   Mike Singletary had been chosen NFL Defensive Player of the
Year. Ditka was soon to be named NFL Coach of the Year. The
Bears were being given early credit for the machine they had
become, yet they had an edge that was sharp and unyielding. And
Jim McMahon—of course—was as surly as ever. He greeted the
press at the Bears' new site by telling assembled members they
basically disgusted him and asking where they were spending New
Year's Eve, so he could avoid that spot. He then added that all of
them were "worried about what everybody thinks. I can give a shit
about what everybody thinks."
   On a cheerier note, Richard Meyer, president of Red Label
Records, which had produced the 23-minute "Super Bowl Shuffle"
video shot at the Park West Theater in Chicago, announced that the
tape had already shipped "triple platinum," and that 550,000
separate audio cassettes had been distributed. Another million of
the things—videos and tapes—were soon to come. The rap, with

the Bears performers in full uniforms, but without helmets and shoulder pads, had shocked everyone by becoming a national hit. Apparently lyrics such as Otis Wilson's "The girls all love me, for my body and my mind," had captivated sports fans throughout the land. Or perhaps it was the refrain—"We're not here to cause no trouble, we're just doin' the Super Bowl Shuffle!"—replete with Fridge's gap-toothed smile and Steve Fuller's pitiful boogeying—that got people excited.

In truth, Fuller had a reason for his ineptitude. The players had filmed the dance the day after the Miami loss (talk about chutzpa), and he was still injured. Aficionados of this kind of thing can study the video closely and notice the bandage still on the hobbling Fuller's foot and ankle. McMahon—"I'm the punky QB"—and Payton had been mixed into the group electronically, since they had done their versions later than the other players. Payton's was done the next day at the Park West, but McMahon's was shot using a blue screen inside a Halas Hall racquetball court. The proceeds of the venture were to be split with the players and various charities—but the accounting, the artists would find out, would be a mess for years.

Not so with game preparation. "Tempers have flared," said Ditka with satisfaction. "Guys are on edge." That was what he wanted, what he felt was needed to complete this journey.

We practiced anywhere during that season. It didn't matter. We had the one grass field behind the offices there in Lake Forest, but the college team would play its games there on Saturdays, and sometimes the field was torn to crap. When it rained or there was lightning, sometimes we'd go into the college gym and run our stuff in sneakers.

But as it got later in the season and the field got more torn up and then frozen solid and we couldn't really accomplish much in a gym, we would go down to South Park, which was about half a mile or so from Halas Hall. It wasn't the location for that cartoon or whatever the hell it is on TV. It was just a neighborhood park. It had tennis courts and jungle gyms and moms walking their babies and dogs sniffing around and all that stuff. But it had a lot of grass, and we could at least run our plays. To get there you had to wind around through the neighborhood and make sure you didn't make a wrong turn and end up in Lake Michigan or Iowa. Guys would commandeer golf carts to get there, or a bunch would jump in the back of the equipment truck and ride along with their legs hanging out. Most everybody else swiped a bike from somewhere or just walked. I guess we should have used the sidewalks, but it was a sleepy suburban neighborhood, so the mighty Chicago Bears would come straggling down the middle of these neighborhood roads, carrying helmets, laughing and goofing around, headed to work.

Kids would come around, and mailmen would honk to get through. It was a sight. Of course, if the McCaskeys had spent a little more money on a bigger place, we wouldn't have had to make our trek. But the Halas Hall facility had been a decent improvement over other NFL sites when it was built in the 1970s, so you couldn't really complain. We played our games at Soldier Field on artificial turf, though, and what we got eventually for practice purposes was a patch of turf about 10 feet by 10 feet on the sideline of our grass field. That really helped. Whoo boy.

But if you're on a mission, what difference does any of it make? It's in your hearts and your heads.

Now it was January, though, and everything in Chicago was frozen like cement. South Park might as well have been a skating rink.

So we went down to Suwanee and practiced before the Giants game, just to keep from freezing to death. That was fine.

Most of the work was done, you see. A team defines itself as a season goes on. You have preseason to get in shape and find the right players, and then you get the offense and defense you want, and then you work to make it come together during the regular season. But you don't suddenly become something you're not. The leopard ain't changing its spots. So you tweak and fine-tune.

Buddy and I were okay again. But the tension, I suppose, would never go away entirely. He was a very stubborn, proud man. And so am I. And he wanted to be a head coach. And why not? So be it. The ending could be what all of us wanted.

One guy who was making some noise was Dennis McKinnon. He wasn't real happy about how little he was being used lately. I loved Dennis, and maybe it's because he was a feisty s.o.b. He didn't weigh much, he was like a slender point guard in basketball, but he would block your ass off downfield or anywhere. Just ask Lawrence Taylor. And he had very soft hands and a knack for getting open and making big plays.

The thing was he'd had arthroscopic knee surgery in early July, and the fact he was back and playing at all was amazing. Football's a tough game, and feelings get hurt. Dennis had seven touchdown catches in the first seven weeks of the season, but in the last seven games he had only seven catches, period, and no TDs. Did that mean he hadn't been a huge part of our team, or wasn't still a huge part? No. But he had to shut up and play, like everybody else. Teamwork. Teamwork. Look, just a few days after my DUI arrest, I had my 46th birthday, and guess what somebody gave me? A "Get Out of Jail Free" card. So I laughed about it. It *was* funny. Embarrassing, but funny. Come on, Dennis. Only three more weeks.

Another guy who had been a tremendous blessing to our team was tight end Tim Wrightman. Everybody always said the Bears couldn't find a tight end ever since old No. 89 moved on,

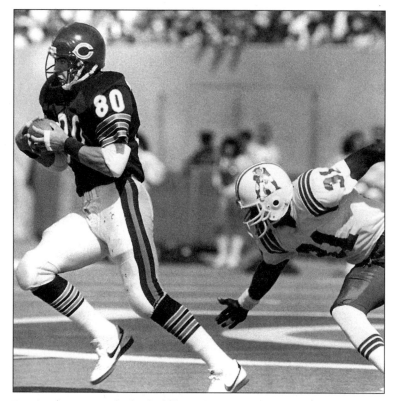

Tim Wrightman was the kind of fill-in tight end we had to have to get where we wanted to go. *Jonathan Daniel/Getty Images*

but Tim did a great job for us. He had a big touchdown catch for us in the Jets game, and he had a streak of at least one catch in eight games, the longest for any receiver on our team. He and Emery Moorehead split a lot of time at tight end, and God knows I loved Emery to death. The stuff he gave us was so much more than a coach would ever count on, and when you get it—you just smile.

Emery was the starter in 14 of our 16 games, and he had been a nobody, just a sixth-round pick by the Giants back in

1977. We got him for nothing, and all he did for us was everything we asked. See, everybody knows about the stars. They glorify the big names. That's all the stupid media does. But players like Moorehead and Wrightman and McKinnon are the foundation of any team. What are you going to do without them? Lose.

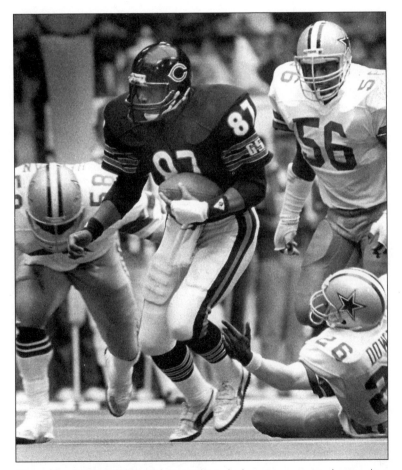

Emery Moorehead was the starting tight end who gave us so much more than we expected. *Jonathan Daniel/Getty Images*

We go back to Chicago for the game, and the city is really cranked up. The lions in front of the Art Institute have Bears helmets on, and all you hear every second of the day is that "Super Bowl Shuffle" thing going on and on. Me, I would rather hear some Sinatra or Nat King Cole, but what the hell. The Fridge rapping, "I'm no dumb cookie," is entertaining, I suppose.

At Soldier Field it's cold and windy, like you'd expect on a January day. People who don't know about the Midwest and the Great Lakes may not have a clue about wind coming in off Lake Michigan or the wind swirling around in places like Cleveland or Buffalo off Lake Erie. In Chicago, Soldier Field is right next to the lake, and the cold wind will come in and do whatever it wants. Sometimes you'll see flags blowing in all four directions. So kickers and quarterbacks better be prepared for it.

Early in the game we back the Giants up toward their own goal at the north end, and it's fourth down. The wind is gusting, and it's something like 14 below zero windchill, but, hell, this is Chicago in the winter, in the playoffs. Get your skirts off. Focus. Forget the damn cold. The snap comes back for Sean Landetta, their punter, and we've got a punt block rush on from the left side with Shaun Gayle and Dennis Gentry. They pick up the rushers, but Landetta is worried or hurried or something, and he goes to punt the ball and he swings his leg as hard as he can and misses it. He misses the freaking ball. Maybe he gets a tiny piece of it, but the wind just moves the ball to the side, and it looked like Charlie Brown trying to kick the ball after Lucy yanks it away.

Gayle picks up the thing at the five and runs it in for a touchdown. We're ahead 7-0, and on this day that's all we're going to need. Our defense is back in its full attack mode. The Giants will rush for a total of 32 yards. And Richard Dent himself will have three and a half sacks for minus-38 yards. Do

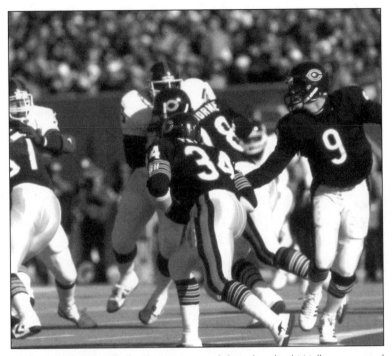

It was cold and windy for the Giants, and then they had Wally to contend with. *Photo by Vernon J. Biever*

the math on that one. McMahon is wearing gloves, which is something I'm not sure I've seen a lot of quarterbacks do, but he throws two touchdown passes to McKinnon. See, I told Dennis to hang in there. The funny thing was, Mac is throwing better spirals than ever. Usually he threw a ball that wobbled around like a wounded duck, but these were almost the way a pro quarterback was supposed to throw.

Yeah, there's wind like in a tornado in the stadium, and Kevin Butler misses every one of his field goal attempts. So I understand how Landetta could screw up like that. But other guys have to step up in these kind of conditions. I told Butthead after the game not to kill himself, to throw the gun away if he had one. It's just a golf shot, I said. It'll come back.

Of course, I was feeling pretty good because we had whipped the Giants and their outstanding coach, Bill Parcells 21-0. Talk about defense. The Giants never converted a third down the entire game. Oh for 12. How could they possibly win? I do recall that Fridge was playing on defense and hit their little running back Joe Morris like a runaway cement truck. Kind of sad when that happens. Otis Wilson had a funny line about it. He said he looked down at Morris, "and I thought it was a poster of him."

Now we were 16-1 and ready for our next step. That would be against the Los Angeles Rams the next Sunday. I was feeling okay, but then the nerves took over again. Where were we now? We were the owners of an amazing record. We were division champs. We had the best defense in the league, the best running back, the best of a lot of things. But we were right back where we were the year before. It was the NFC championship game coming up, against another West Coast team. I couldn't take another game like the San Francisco game from last season. And I knew guys like Payton and Singletary couldn't, either.

Or a guy like free safety Gary Fencik. He was a Yale guy who had his MBA from Northwestern, and you would probably think he was some yuppie pinhead sissy who didn't give a damn and just wanted to look pretty. But he was another ferocious guy. Hell, coming into 1985 he already had more tackles than any Bear ever, even Dick Butkus. He and Doug Plank used to run into receivers just for fun. Just to see if they could knock them out.

Fencik was writing a column for one of the newspapers, which was appropriate because he was the brains of our defense. In that NFC game out in San Francisco in 1984 Gary had four tackles, an assist, two passes broken up, and two interceptions.

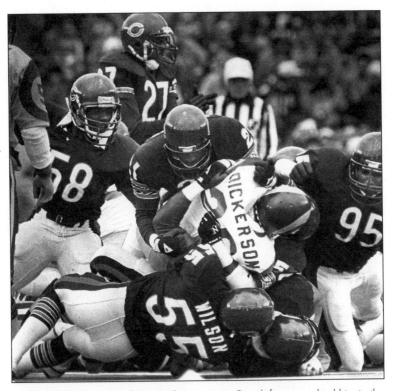

It didn't matter how good Eric Dickerson was. Our defense crushed him in the
NFC title game. *Jonathan Daniel/Getty Images*

If we'd won, he probably would have been MVP. If we'd won.
Fencik didn't want to go out like Ernie Banks, like Gayle Sayers,
like Jerry Sloan, like Ron Santo, or any of those other Chicago
stars who had never won the championship game.

We were everybody's biggest target, including, I'm sure, the
Rams. A lot of people loved us, but I think a lot of people hated
us, too. Maybe I'm wrong about that. I was really a guy with
blinders on at that time, not caring about the rest of the world.
Just our own little world.

The genius oddsmakers had made us 10-point favorites over L.A., but they didn't have to play. The Rams had Eric Dickerson at tailback, and he was one of the best runners in the history of the NFL. In their last game he'd run for 248 yards. I respected their coach, John Robinson, too. He'd come to the NFL after coaching at Southern Cal and taking them to three Rose Bowl championships in seven years. But deep down inside I felt this year was different. Yeah, we were playing another huge game to see if we could get into the Super Bowl. But this time we were playing it at home. We were the top dogs in this one. That's right, all of those regular-season wins weren't just for show. They meant something.

Then, too, L.A. was starting a guy named Dieter Brock at quarterback, a 34-year-old rookie, who had come into the NFL from the Canadian League. I'm sorry, but with our defense, that was like throwing a pork chop into a dog pound. I may have told our team that. I'm sure Buddy did. But we didn't say anything publicly.

I started talking about us being the Grabowskis. I meant it. We were the common man. And now the common man was going to do something the fancy man could only hope to do.

The game started, and it was a cold, gray day, and I remember it looked like it could snow at any second.

McMahon had been fined by the NFL front office $5,000 for wearing a headband that said "adidas" on in it during a previous game. I don't know why he wore it. Probably to make money. So in this game he's got the adidas thing around his neck, and when he takes his helmet off I see he's got a new stretchy thing around his forehead. This one says, "ROZELLE." Jesus, there's no explaining this guy. I mean, Pete Rozelle is the freaking commissioner of the league. And he's at the game, watching.

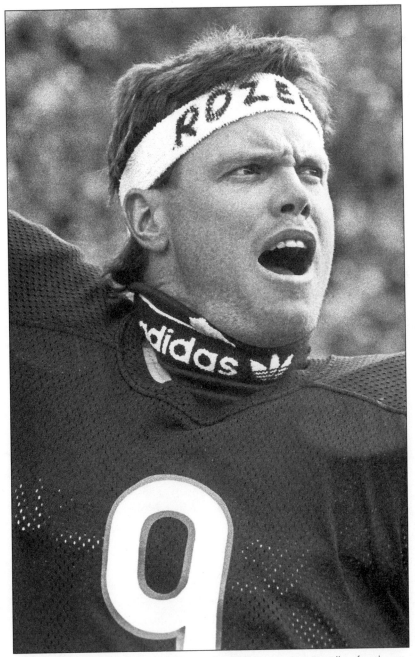

Mac shows his love for Chicago fans and commissioner Pete Rozelle after the win over the Rams. *Jonathan Daniel/Getty Images*

But I suppose it was sort of fun, and I heard later Rozelle loved it. It was pretty clever, I suppose, and about the most interesting thing McMahon could do after being ordered not to wear signs on his head.

You need discipline on a team, but as I've said all along, McMahon was a different duck. He was the most devious person in the world, and he'd always find a way to get under your skin. Mine, Rozelle's, the opponents', everybody's. To be honest, though, I think Walter sometimes wore a headband that said "Kangaroo" on it, a shoe company that gave him a car when he broke Jim Brown's all-time rushing record. They paid him a lot of money, so why shouldn't he advertise their company? I just don't like the way the league lets guys make idiots of themselves in all of these end zone things, all of these dumb-ass celebrations, and then uses it to promote the NFL. Why should they care what your helmet or T-shirt says? You know why? They're not getting their cut of the money. That's why it bothers them. You want to straighten things out, then cut out everything—all of the promotion. Just make it football. Is that asking too much?

I mean, right now the NFL won't let the 49ers' new coach, Mike Nolan, wear a suit on the sideline. They said they'd fine him, because he has to wear official NFL issue. That's just flat-out embarrassing to the NFL. Mike Nolan's dad, Dick, was a great coach in the league, and he wore a suit, and his son is trying to honor him. It's disrespectful to Tom Landry, to Vince Lombardi, to Buddy Parker, hell, to George Halas. They all wore suits on the sideline. The NFL is all about marketing now, not being reasonable.

One reason I'm such a Mike Nolan fan is he hired one of my favorite players for his staff, one of my favorite people in life, Mike Singletary. Another one of my favorites, Les Frazier, is also coaching in the NFL under Tony Dungy in Indianapolis. Les was one of the most underrated cornerbacks ever. He had six interceptions in that 1985 season, and he would get another one off Brock against the Rams. Nice guy, and I'm thrilled he's a coach. And Singletary—you know how I feel, and I'll tell you more about him in a minute.

But thinking about individualism always brings me back to McMahon. He had a great ability to recognize defenses, and when he saw something he knew was wrong or weak, he knew how to exploit it. But the main thing is he was not at all reluctant to audible after he saw something. Didn't care at all. Avellini and Harbaugh would put me over the edge with a couple of terrible audibles, but McMahon did it all of the time. And I gave him the freedom to do it. Sometimes I didn't understand why I did. But I did. And as a result of that he made some incredible plays for us that year. I guess that's what a creative madman can do if given a chance.

That's what he did early in the first quarter. We were down in the red zone, and it was third and eight, and we had a pass play called. McMahon scrambled to his left and faked, looked for receivers, faked, and then he took off running. He got a couple blocks downfield, and this beat-up guy weaved around and dove into the end zone for a 16-yard touchdown. Hell, the great Eric Dickerson's longest run of the day was nine yards. And no TDs, either.

Then with the score 10-0 in the third quarter, we have the ball again, and it is second and 10 at the Rams' 22. I call a draw play. Give it to Wally, see what he could do. Seems like a no-brainer. But there's McMahon at the line looking around, barking off stuff. Oh Jesus, I know something's happening. He's calling an audible. There's the snap, and McMahon moves to his left. Willie Gault is lined up on the left and he runs downfield and gives an inside fake to cornerback LeRoy Irvin, a beautiful post-flag move, and Irvin bites on it, and Jim throws a perfect

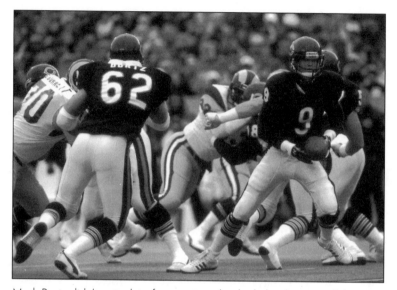

Mark Bortz didn't get a lot of recognition, but he helped us pound the Rams to get to the "Ultimate Game." *Photo by Vernon J. Biever*

touchdown pass to Willie in the corner of the end zone. Jim's feet were off the ground when he threw and he was all cockeyed, and his arm went straight across his body, exactly how nobody should ever do it.

I'm a genius, aren't I?

McMahon was pumped up. I remember what Payton said afterward. "He was a crazy nut out there. He did everything but take his clothes off, and if we'd been out there longer, he might have done that."

Seventeen points was way more than we needed, because the defense had locked down the Rams offense and thrown away the key. Dickerson got a total of 46 yards rushing, and Brock threw for a total of 44 net yards. It was a joke! They had 130 total yards of offense, and our defense even outscored them.

The defensive touchdown came with under three minutes left, and the crowd really started to get excited, realizing we might truly make it this year. Singletary had been playing his usual great game, and I could see that warrior look of determination in his eyes. They didn't call him "Samurai" for nothing. This was a guy who was so intense and focused on being a great football player that at Baylor he broke 16 of his own helmets. During the Rams game he saw some screws lying on the field and didn't realize they came from his own head gear, and his facemask was ready to drop off. He broke his chinstrap after that. And at the end his helmet was cracked. He didn't care.

At one practice in 1984 he was leading the team in calisthenics and he just started screaming, "I refuse to go home early! I refuse to go home early!" Can you understand how much this guy wanted it? All of it?

Well, he wasn't going home early this year. Dieter Brock dropped back to pass, and Buddy's dogs came roaring in on him, just like they had all afternoon. Dent smacked the ball away, and Brock went flying. William Perry came lumbering by and tried to pick up the loose ball. It kept bouncing, and finally Wilbur Marshall got it. He shrugged off Dickerson, who was diving for him, and then he took off upfield. Fridge was running with him like a big old elephant, and some other Bears were all around, looking back, like a posse. Singletary must have been somewhere in there, I know he was, and my God, it was beautiful. It had just started snowing, these big, slow flakes coming down like in one of those Christmas snow globes, and it was perfect. Bears weather, Bears dominance, Bears success, Bears kicking ass. If we could have frozen that scene and made it a billboard, it would have captured the season.

We won 24-0. In our two playoff games we had scored 45 points and hadn't given up one.

There were cigars in the locker room, brought by Covert. But it was still subdued. No champagne, no screaming. Lots of hugs, handshakes. Big smiles. But we had one more rung to climb, one more peak. Everybody knew that.

Of course, McMahon said what was on his mind.

"Fuck the champagne, I want a beer."

Chapter Fourteen

Cannons Don't Fall out of Trees

It was on to New Orleans for the Bears for Super Bowl XX.

Their opponent was the New England Patriots, who had won the AFC championship by upsetting the Dolphins 31-14 in Miami. That score was a shocker, but Pats quarterback Tony Eason had been remarkably efficient in the game, completing 10 of 12 passes for three touchdowns. The Bears had beaten the Patriots 20-7 in the second game of the season, as everyone distantly recalled. It seemed like years ago. And in truth, over four months had gone by since that hot day at Soldier Field. Teams change. They learn, they peak, they flourish, they wane. There are injuries. Luck grows. It runs out. But the Bears could not fear the Patriots. The wreckage they had just caused in the playoffs was unprecedented. Nobody had tossed two shutouts before. Fear the Pats? As much as they feared Pat the Bunny.

Ditka had warned his team about getting complacent, however. He didn't want the players getting caught up in the hype. He didn't want them getting overwhelmed. He wanted them even-keeled, in their fashion. He quoted what his former Dallas Cowboys teammate Duane Thomas had once said to Super Bowl reporters: "If this is the ultimate game, why do they play one next year?"

Before the Bears actually traveled to New Orleans, however, they visited the now-completed bubble in Champaign, Illinois, staying for a week of pre-New Orleans week intensity on the University of Illinois campus. They had things to work on, because everyone said the Patriots had improved since the start of the year. Well, they had to improve. Indeed, the Pats finished up leading the AFC in takeaways with 47 and then got a stunning 16 more in their three playoff games. On offense Eason had been hurt in the sixth game, and the offense was handed to veteran quarterback Steve Grogan. New England had flourished under Grogan, winning its next six games, before Grogan himself was injured. Eason took over the starting role once more, but the Patriots did not

*falter under him this time. They continued on with their improved
running game and an opportunistic, attacking defense.*

*The Bears tuned their defense in Champaign and set in motion
Ditka's plan for offensive attack: be aggressive; take chances; be
prepared to use Payton as a decoy if the Patriots made stopping him
their sole focus. Whatever—never make the same mistake as in last
year's NFC championship game. Do not sit back and let things
happen.* Make *them happen.*

*Buddy Ryan had been rumored to have been talking with the
Philadelphia Eagles about their head coaching position, but he
denied it. "I'm more excited about getting ready for the Super
Bowl," he said. "That's what my mind's on right now."*

*Ryan's defense had finished the regular season ranked first in
the NFL in turnovers, yards allowed, and points allowed.
Everything that meant anything. "It would be an irreplaceable loss
to this team," said Singletary of Ryan's possible departure. "It would
take a long time to recover from his loss." The middle linebacker
continued on in his somber, impassioned tone. "He's more than a
coach. He's a leader, a father, and a friend."*

*Oh, and McMahon was injured once more. This time it was
his lower back and upper buttocks. He was injured when he slid
feet first in the Rams game, a signal for the defense to lay off, and
still was steam-rolled by a defender. "I got a serious pain in the ass
right now," is how Jimmy Mac gently put it.*

I was thinking about the class of 1983 when I looked at this
team, all the rookies who joined the team in what was my
second year as coach. That was some year for our draft. Eight of
the guys we picked were starters—Jim Covert, Willie Gault,
Dave Duerson, Tom Thayer, Richard Dent, Mark Bortz, Mike
Richardson, and Dennis McKinnon. I mean, those are good
players. You can say what you want about coaching and schemes
and all that, but you need the horses to run the race. Ask any

coach at the elite level, and if he's truthful, he'll say, "Yeah, we had the studs." We had ours. I'm the first to admit it. I had the best football players on the best team I'd ever seen. We went off to New Orleans feeling confident, to say the least.

I had told all the guys from the beginning of the year that the only thing that would be acceptable to me, to all of us, was to win the Super Bowl. It was a progression that we had to hold to. Develop a good team, develop the offense, the defense, develop the bonds, the teamwork, move forward, and when we got there, grab it all. Coming close would mean nothing now. We had been close. And I looked at that Dolphins game, that 38-24 loss. They weren't better than us. We stunk that day. I would have loved to have played them in the Super Bowl, to kick their ass, just to show everybody. But the Patriots beat them before we got a chance. So what can you do?

That *Monday Night* game haunted me, to be honest. Miami couldn't have beaten us unless we didn't adjust to their offense. They weren't a better team than we were. I salute them for beating us, but they weren't nearly as good as we were. We had to do nothing to compensate for their offense for them to win. And we did. I'll tell Buddy Ryan that, I'll tell anybody that. I'll go to my grave saying we played stupid defensive football.

What we did now was, we got all our work accomplished in Champaign. We studied and prepared and ran our drills, and we had our game plan laid out like a map. It was something I learned when I was with the Cowboys. I learned it from Tom Landry. Dallas went to a lot of Super Bowls, and there had always been two weeks between the NFC championship game and the final game. Tom put everything in that was needed in week one. He said then when you get down there you can tune it, you can tweak it. But you don't rebuild it. Super Bowl weeks are crazy enough. Why try to fight it? I mean, you know who the other team is, what they do. They've just done it for 18 games. They're not suddenly going to turn into something they've never been. You can get into a lot of trouble by trying to reinvent the wheel.

You know your players. You believe in what you've been doing. They believe in it. When we finally packed up and flew to New Orleans we had the right philosophy and the right feeling, and we never changed a damn thing once we got there.

We were not all perfect friends, don't get me wrong. As I may have mentioned, I don't believe Hampton and McMahon ever got along very well. They never really had a love for each other, and I don't know why that is. They were both the same kind of player, they just played on opposite sides of the ball. Dan gave everything he had, every down, every breath. He had knee problems and he was always beaten up, but it never stopped him. That's why he's in the Hall of Fame. McMahon, I think what you have to understand about him—whether you love him or hate him—is that he was one of the most competitive people on the planet. He wasn't acting like somebody he wasn't. If we were losing, you might have thought he was an egomaniac. But I can honestly say I don't think Jim McMahon ever cared more about himself than about the team. He did some strange things to draw attention to himself, but it never affected his teammates or his play.

There we were on our way to the Super Bowl, and naturally, stuff was happening everywhere. Again, I wasn't paying much attention to anything outside of the team and the preparation. McMahon had been on David Letterman, then Bob Hope, Fridge was doing stuff, everybody wanted Payton, there were posters. The damned "Super Bowl Shuffle" never ended. But I was worried a bit about Stanley Morgan, one of the Patriots' wide receivers. He may have been 30 years old, but he had the highest yards-per-reception average of any active NFL player, almost 21 yards a catch. He didn't catch a million balls, only 39 during the season, but he was dangerous as hell when he did.

Then there was their other wideout, a young guy named Irving Fryar. Yeah, the media was watching us, and I suppose we gave them a lot to watch. But Fryar was getting watched, too. He'd missed the AFC championship game because he'd badly cut his ring finger and sliced the tendon in the little finger of his right hand. The news stories said he'd been in a fight with his pregnant wife and there was a knife, and, well, something happened. Besides catching passes, he was New England's leading punt returner. Hell, he was the leading punt returner in the NFL. Their safety Roland James replaced him against the Dolphins and fumbled twice. And a guy named Stephen Starring had replaced Fryar at wideout, and he didn't have a catch in the game. It mattered a bit to us whether Fryar played or not. Although, with our defense, maybe not that much.

New England coach Raymond Berry came out with some nice coach-speak. "I'm not sure that Starring isn't every bit as good as Fryar," he said.

Good work, Ray.

The main thing was, in my mind, Tony Eason was not Dan Marino. Raymond Berry is one of my favorite friends, a guy I respect and love to death. But Don Shula had realized before that 13th game that our offense was what it was, maybe he thought he could stop it. Maybe not. But the Dolphins weren't terribly worried about our offense, at any rate. It was our defense that terrified them. So Shula went after it. He spent his time trying to beat our defense. Why could he do that? Because he had Dan Marino. Guys like Marino don't fall out of trees. Dan Marino has a cannon that God hands out to maybe one person a century. And he didn't give one to Tony Eason.

I told the players again about Duane Thomas and the Super Bowl. As a player I sat near Duane in the Dallas locker room, and I didn't know him well—he was real hard to understand and be a tight friend with. He was aloof and silent a lot. But he was a lot smarter than I thought.

Here's hoping we could be smart, too.

Chapter Fifteen

Stick a Needle in This

The circus packed its tents, herded the giraffes and tigers onto the flatcars, rousted up the fat man and the bearded ladies and the jugglers and the strongmen and headed down to New Orleans. There had been other eccentric and entertaining, even evil or nearly sanctified teams in the 19 previous Super Bowls, but there had never been a carnival like the Chicago Bears. You had dark Raiders and be-haloed Cowboys in the past. But here was something for everyone.

From the riveting talent of Walter Payton to the intensity of the defensive line, to the pulpit frenzy of Mike Singletary to the splendor of William "The Refrigerator" Perry to the antisocial unpredictability of Jim McMahon, you could spend hours observing the Bears, and still have room for popcorn. And in the end it was all because there had never been a head coach like Mike Ditka.

Ditka's zeal was renowned, but who ever thought the wild man from western Pennsylvania would lead a band of disparate souls to the pinnacle of team sports? It was fascinating to all to know that Ditka was behind this thing, not as a player, but as a coach. See how people could change? Or maybe change wasn't necessary, only tweaking, only passion. Ditka seemed so unlike Hank Stram or Chuck Noll or Bill Walsh or, of course, Tom Landry, as to be another species. But maybe not.

McMahon's butt was still sore, of course, and he wanted his acupuncturist, a fellow named Hiroshi Shiriashi, to be flown to New Orleans to stick pins in his posterior. This created a minor brouhaha and much debate in the media and rowdy sports bars about the benefits of and philosophy behind Eastern healing processes. Ditka didn't care if somebody stuck a bazooka up McMahon's ass. If it calmed the quarterback down, eased his discomfort, and helped him play, do it. Willie Gault, ever the avant garde health savant, wanted the acupuncturist brought in, too, to work on him.

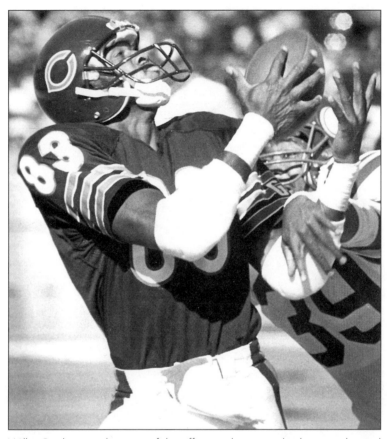

Willie Gault was a big part of the offensive threat—maybe because he and McMahon shared an acupuncturist. *Jonathan Daniel/Getty Images*

Shortly after the ruckus began, Bears president Michael McCaskey, who had barred the acupuncturist from flying on the team's charter plane, said fine, enough, I give. "We're going to welcome him with a brass band," McCaskey, the foppish chief, said sarcastically. Shiriashi and another specialist were flown to the bayou by the Illinois State Acupuncture Association—hey, this was where the publicity was!—and the needles came out.

McMahon himself was peeved with the press, generally, telling the assembled masses on Media Monday at the Superdome, that the stupid scrutiny "comes with winning. I don't think too many of you guys are up in Green Bay right now." He may have casually stuffed another gob of tobacco into his lower lip as he said this.

Back in Chicago Mayor Harold Washington declared that the Daley Center Plaza was now "Bears Plaza," and had workers erect a complex 600-square-foot television screen, consisting of 28,000 tiny tubes, that showed—what else?—the "Super Bowl Shuffle" on a continual loop. Folks everywhere lapped up the mid-winter zaniness.

William Perry was asked about women fans, whether they wrote to him, maybe sent photos? "I don't get no letters from no ladies," Fridge declared sternly. Steve McMichael told the media about clearing out biker bars with Dan Hampton, about whatever deranged things came to his crafty mind. Asked by reporters about his snake-hunting hobby, how he lured the snakes, McMichael drawled for their amusement, "You throw a reporter out there, and when the rattlesnake bites, you just grab it behind the neck."

Pete Rozelle declared of the Bears, speaking for the universe, or at least the TV-aware NFL, "We love them. They got a 75 rating for the Rams game."

The Bears were on the cover of Time *magazine.*

They were officially the rage.

The truth is we were nervous and concerned, but we also were confident as hell. As Dennis McKinnon told the media, if we don't make mistakes, there's no way in hell the Patriots can beat us. That was just the plain truth. Hampton said we didn't want to squeak by, we wanted to beat them soundly. And we did want to. We were favored by 10 points or something, but I thought that if we did what we were capable of, we could win big, really make a statement.

Otis Wilson even said we wanted a shutout. Fine. We did.
But let's not talk too much. Their guy Raymond Clayborn said
he thought Wilson "was crazy," and he added, "Obviously, it
will be an incentive for our offense to prove them wrong. And
I know they will." Clayborn played defensive back. I don't think
he knew much about our defense. He'd never played against it.
I think he should have asked, oh, let's say the Giants or Rams
about it. But that was fine. Who cared about Raymond
Clayborn? It was all just talk.

There was a flu bug going around down in New Orleans,
and I don't just mean from Bourbon Street hangovers. Tony
Eason had a case of it, Kevin Butler missed Friday's practice and
was hospitalized because of it, and some coaches and other
people didn't feel too hot. But this was the biggest game of most
people's lives, so, I mean, are you going to miss it because of a
virus?

There were people coming and telling me they saw
McMahon out on Bourbon Street at 2:30 in the morning. And,
no, I didn't have a curfew until Saturday, the night before the
game. But we had wakeup calls at 6:30 in the morning, and if
the guys didn't know what was really important just now, they
were pretty messed up.

Chicago teams always seemed to crumble when they were
close to winning it all. The 1969 Cubs had done it, then the
1984 Cubs did. The White Sox blew the Series in 1959. The
Bears had that 1963 NFL championship, the one I played on,
but that was 22 years ago, and it wasn't the Super Bowl. Getting
close didn't mean jack to me. You practice and work so you can
get close. Then you take close and you kick its carcass to hell.
You want the top, the championship. You smell it, you taste it.
You get it. That's all there is.

McMahon's acupuncture guy showed up, and Jim and
Willie got worked on. Got stuck with more pins than a voodoo

doll, I guess. The press asked me about McMahon's butt on Wednesday, and I said it was 200 percent better. Was it? I don't know. Jesus, I was supposed to be monitoring his ass?

I just knew he was going to play. I mean, McMahon even wore a headband that said, "ACUPUNCTURE" on it. I just hoped everyone would make it to game time. McMahon supposedly had pushed a photographer who was trying to take his picture in the French Quarter. Now that I think about it, maybe I did have a curfew after that. But I wasn't going around and knocking on guys' doors.

Myself, I wasn't partying. I got a touch of the flu and took it easy at night. I really didn't feel too well the whole week. My parents were in town, and we went out to dinner one night, Diana and my folks, but that was about it. My kids were there, too. I waited in the Hilton Hotel is all I did. Otis, meanwhile, was still talking, but that's because the press kept asking questions. I think they'd ask dumb-ass questions until they took their last little breath. "The Rams are better than the Patriots," Otis told them. "I don't think there's any comparison." There probably wasn't.

People were asking about the weather, and if it might affect us. We're playing in a freaking dome. Honest to God, that happened. Then on Wednesday a helicopter flies over when we're practicing outdoors at the New Orleans Saints' practice field in Metairie, Louisiana. It hovers overhead, taking photos or whatever, and next thing you know, McMahon has dropped his shorts and is mooning the camera crew, showing them his hurt butt cheeks. Next day in the papers, there he is, doing his thing. What can I say? Shame on you? Yes, I cared, because I thought it was an embarrassment to the organization. People would look at us and say we're idiots. Maybe we were to a degree. But I wouldn't call attention to the fact. Jim was wrong there. A little discretion might be in order. I wasn't thrilled. But

How smart is the media? Here it is pre-Super Bowl, soaking up everything Jimmy Mac can spout. *Jonathan Daniel/Getty Images*

would I go to the wall for him as my starting quarterback? Absolutely.

For us as a team, the main thing was we never changed our philosophy in New Orleans. It started in Platteville, and we believed in what we were doing. You don't take risks if you don't have to, but if you don't risk something, you have no chance.

We risked being aggressive, That's what we were. That's what we would remain.

The night before the game we had meetings. Basically, that's it. I met with the whole team, and I told them you're not winning this game for me or for Halas or McCaskey or anybody else. You're winning it for yourselves, for the guy sitting next to you. It's not about anything I've ever said. You have this wonderful moment in time, and you can answer to each other forever.

I had some of the guys stand up and say what the game meant to them. We broke it up then and I talked to the offense, and Buddy talked to the defense in another room. I guess their part got pretty crazy. They might have gone nuts. There was a lot of noise, and I think maybe a projector got smashed and maybe there were some holes in the wall. I think Buddy told the players he loved them and he was leaving, taking that Eagles job. I don't know for sure. But that's what he told me later. And they knew something was over, this was it. Their general had one more battle. The defense had its bayonettes fixed. I know that.

I went to bed early. Sunday was a blur. With a game starting so late, it was like a *Monday Night* game, and that just messes with you. All day long you have to wait around. And here we are so close to the Superdome that we can walk there. No need to leave early or anything. I know I got up around 5 a.m. or earlier, and we had Mass for the Catholics and devotionals for the Protestants, and we got the position coaches together for a while. But it was really nothing. We try to eat our pregame meal three or four hours before game time, so we did that, but I don't remember many details. It's all such a cloud of anticipation. I do know I was thinking constantly that two teams get to these championships and nobody remembers the team that loses.

That's crazy, if you think about it.

We're 17-1, but if we finish 17-2, it's nothing. I had too much time to think. You get too much time, you get pregnant with ideas. But I had watched so much film of the Patriots, I knew the whole defense would key on Payton, and why not? So what a great weapon that was. And what a great decoy he could be.

The thing is our defense hadn't been scored on in the playoffs, and to say we were confident was an understatement. Still, you don't know. You don't know. Damn, you just don't know. The clock would not move.

After what seemed like years, the game finally started. Actually, it almost began, and then it was delayed a little bit because of too much smoke from the fireworks inside the Superdome or something. Noise, screaming, cameras everywhere. Everybody was uptight. Even McMahon. We got the ball, and on the second play Jim called the wrong formation on a weak side slant, and Walter got hit just when he was getting the ball and he fumbled. The Patriots recovered at our 19-yard line. Oh, this is a great way to start. This is perfect.

McMahon had had his butt shot up by team doctor Clarence Fossier, probably with novocaine and a little cortisone in there. He also was wearing gloves. Indoors. Help me. He told me he was going to do it. He'd worn them in the last two games, which were cold as hell, but here it's 72 degrees, maybe hotter. I said, "Is that the right thing to do?"

"I get a better grip on the ball," he said.

"Okay," I said. "Do whatever you want."

But when he came to the sideline now, I said, "What are you *doing?*"

"I messed up," he said. "I called the wrong formation."

When he called a Slant 24, it should have gone left to the weak side, instead of to the right. Maybe he got confused for an instant by the numbers, because, see, I numbered even to the left and odd to the right, which nobody else does. That was from Coach Landry. . . .

But this is the thing—our defense didn't let New England move forward an inch after the turnover, not a single inch, and they had to settle for a field goal from the same spot. Talk about character. We had become a whole.

And the rout was on.

We scored the next 44 points. It was an ass-whipping. Plain and simple. Everything we knew we could do, we did. I don't think I've ever been prouder of a game plan in my life. They keyed on Walter like we thought they would, and so we used him in motion or flanked him or used him as a decoy and let

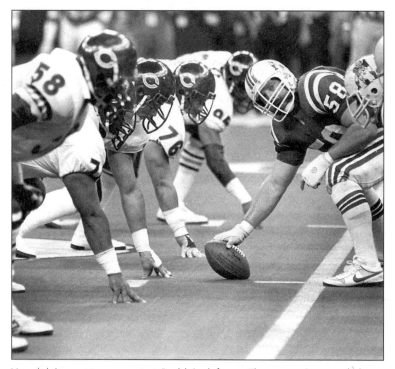

You didn't want to go against Buddy's defense. There wasn't an audible on the planet that could help you. *Photo by Vernon J. Biever*

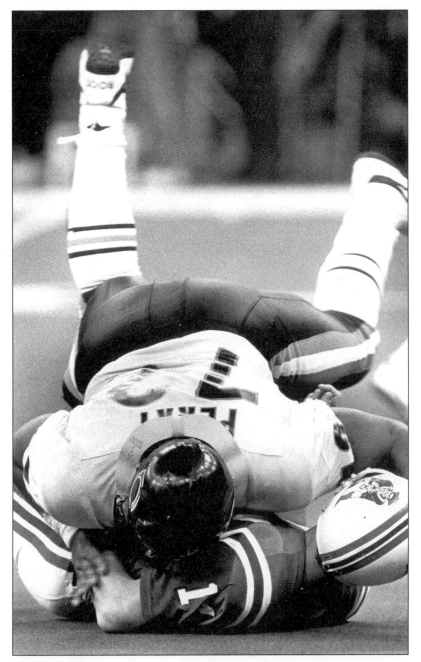

Steve Grogan finds out what it feels like when a refrigerator lands on you.
Jonathan Daniel/Getty Images

Suhey carry the ball. We hit them with so many missiles it was unreal. The first time we got the ball back, we hit them with a 43-yard pass to Gault. I wasn't going to play it tight. I knew going in this was balls to the wall.

Butler had two field goals early, then Suhey scored on an 11-yard run. It was only 23-3 at the half, but we were killing them. They had minus-14 yards of total offense for the half. We were making them go *backward*.

In the third quarter we scored two touchdowns to make it 37-3. Then we had the ball at their one, and I sent in Fridge. He plowed it over to make the score 44-3. I'd already put him in to block once and also to pass. That didn't work, and he got tackled while still looking to throw. He is probably the heaviest man ever to be sacked.

Tony Eason, I'm not blaming him, but I think our defense was so relentless that he got shell-shocked. I think he started looking for the rush, for who was going to earhole him or hit his back or his knees or slam him, and he couldn't concentrate on routes or receivers. I mean, wow, he did not complete a single pass in the game. He was zero-for-eight, oh for the Super Bowl. Steve Grogan came in later, but it was history. We annihilated the Patriots 46-10. Richard Dent was the MVP, and that was a great choice. He represented that incredible defense.

McMahon played well after that first series, with two touchdown runs and 256 yards passing. He wore all of these headbands, too, looked like a street sign, but he was very clever about it. One said "Plato" or "Pluto" or something like that, for a friend of his, one was for juvenile diabetes and one said "POW-MIA" for the war veterans. Not that I was watching his forehead. But this, I found out later, was famous stuff. This was what got the media excited.

When it was over, when the final second ran off, I felt this incredible sense of relief. The hype and the buildup had been so

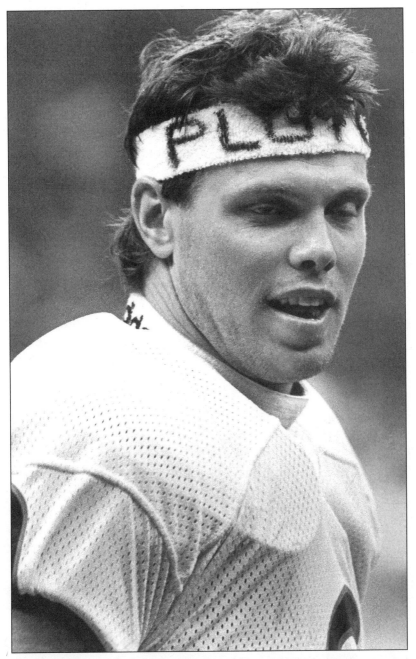

More headband craziness from McMahon in New Orleans. This time it said "Pluto" for a friend of his, not the actual planet. *Photo by Vernon J. Biever*

huge, that I just felt totally drained. I didn't even notice the guys coming to pick me up. Some players grabbed Buddy and hoisted him up, and two guys got me. Looking at photos now, I see it was McMichael with my right leg and Fridge with my left. It scared me a bit, to tell you the truth. I'd never been lifted like that before. My hips and legs aren't in mint condition, you know. But it was a great feeling, too. Two defensive players were picking me up, although Fridge was part of the offense, too, of course. As I recall, they were very gentle.

I was glad I got to have some fun with William Perry. I did the stuff with him, because he was a good player and I liked him. I was going to have him run for a touchdown, catch one, and throw one. It almost worked. I probably would have let him kick a field goal, too. Nah, I wouldn't have. I wouldn't have let Walter kick one. There were limits. People said I told William, "I made you a hero," but I never said that. We just had a good time, that's all.

But what I realized after the game, after we were champions, 18-1, and bigshots of the day, was that Walter Payton didn't score in the game. And that bothered him. And because it bothered him, it bothered me. McMahon had two short TD runs. Perry had one. Suhey had one. Walter had none. I didn't plan that. That put a damper on things later. I asked Walter, and he said it didn't bother him, but it did. I regret not giving him that honor. But we had a game plan, and he was the whole reason it worked, because wherever he went, the Patriots defense went. Later I explained this to him. I don't think he ever accepted it totally.

The other thing I regret is Les Frazier blowing out his knee on a reverse on a punt return. He was a defensive back used to running backward. Now he's carrying the ball, going forward? I love Steve Kazor, our special teams coach, but I don't know if

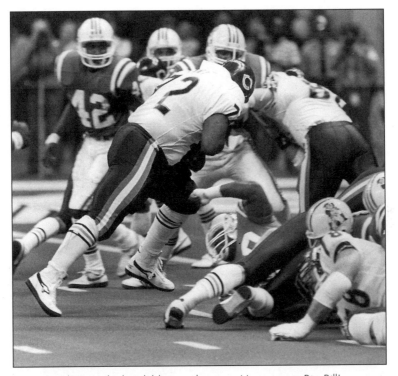

Super Bowl XX. Hide the children and pizzas. Here comes Big Bill!
Photo by Vernon J. Biever

that was necessary. It was a freak thing, but Les was never really the same afterward.

I mean, think about it. A bench kid named Keith Ortego—a guy wearing my No. 89, by the way—signals a fair catch and then grabs the ball and runs and hands off to Les. There's a penalty flag, and the play doesn't even count. Frazier was one of the best cornerbacks in the NFL, and he'll never get credit for it, because he didn't have a long career, and he wasn't a showboat like Deion Sanders. And at his highest peak, at our moment of glory, he goes down like that. I guess that's football.

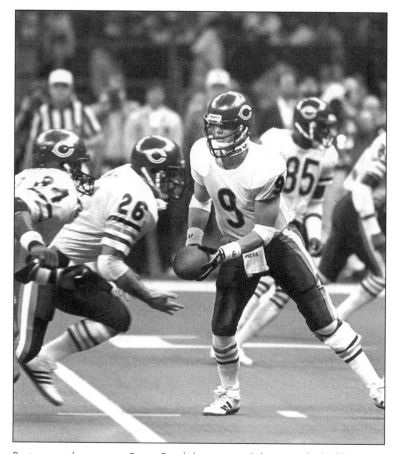

Payton was the greatest Super Bowl decoy ever. Suhey gets the ball because the Patriots' defense moved everywhere Walter did. *Photo by Vernon J. Biever*

Life is fragile. You never know. My buddy and teammate Joe Marconi died young. You wonder why some go and some stay. Why do things happen? It was so good for Marconi, then boom—dead at 54. Everybody knows about the tragedy of Brian Piccolo. And I am always haunted by Farrington and Galimore in that crash.

You have to appreciate things at the moment and never stop trying to achieve what you want. I just read that a guy I played against, Jim Otto, is in danger of losing his leg. He never missed a game in 15 years, but he's had over 50 major surgeries because of his injuries, and he has so many artificial joints that his body's immunity to infection is gone. It's a tragedy. It's like old George Connor of the Bears who went through stuff like that.

Jim Otto was a warrior. Back then we played hurt. Sports medicine sure wasn't what it is now. And you didn't want to have your job taken from you, the way Wally Pipp got his taken by Lou Gehrig. See, you get in the starting blocks and you run the race. That's what you do. That's what George Connor did. That's life. You can't rewrite things as you go along. You have to go straight ahead on the path you've chosen, with all your might. Who is Jim Otto? All those things. *That's* who he is.

Me, I wouldn't change anything. I had that groin problem, and they shot me up all the time with cortisone back in the day, so deep it went to my hip socket, and I think that's why it wore out. They say you should get cortisone a couple times a year, tops, and I was getting two or three shots a week. And the dislocated foot I got when a guy fell on it back in the early 1960s, that caused a lot of other things to go. I remember Dr. Fox, the old Bears doctor, put it in a cast in training camp. But I'm "Iron Mike," so I'm out dancing every night. He takes the cast off after a month and he says, "That doesn't look very good." I take a step and fall down.

I don't think he did anything. I don't think he did anything but put a cast on it. Later a doctor said he could fix my foot, but he'd have to break about eight bones to do it. And I played the whole season on it. Never got it fixed. Fox is the guy who messed up Dick Butkus's leg, too. But I loved the guy. What the hell, I don't know. You didn't sue medical people back then. I sure wasn't going to. You're the player. He's the doctor. Play ball.

I was sorry about Todd Bell and Al Harris not being part of that Super Bowl season. But they got bad advice. In life, that happens. And it was true that Richard Dent was underpaid at $90,000. And he should be in the Hall of Fame. But where else was he going to make that kind of money? And whether I'm right or wrong, this is about team. And we were a team. Who knows what would have happened if you go back and change a thing here or a thing there? Maybe if Todd and Al had been on the team we wouldn't have won. That's why you do what you feel you have to do, with what you've got.

It's cold and it's cruel, this life. But it's great, too. It's all there together.

Take that movie I was in. There I am playing myself, smoking a cigar, and who's next to me? Why, it's Will Ferrell, one of the funniest guys in the world. He came to my bar one night and he did the greatest Harry Caray you've ever heard. Diana and I were dying. And who's on the other side? Why, it's Robert Duvall, who may be a better actor even than Robert DeNiro. Why me with these guys? I don't know. Nobody knows.

• • • • •

So there we were, champions of the world. Maybe I thought about luck a little when I popped my head up through the sun roof of that limo, there in downtown Chicago. How lucky I've been. But damn, it was cold. Beautiful, in a frozen way. What a place for a parade, especially one that wasn't moving.

I hadn't slept much, but that wind was a nice slap to the face. All those thousands and thousands of people cheering. It was wonderful. And yet, on Tuesday, less than 48 hours after we won, the space shuttle blew up. That put things in perspective. We didn't visit the White House like we were supposed to because of that. We were about the only winning Super Bowl team that never got to do that.

But for one moment in time, one fleeting second, we were the best in the world. In that moment we were the best of all, because we had beaten down our opponents, fair and square. And if you don't play to beat the best, to beat them all, why play?

I can say I came full circle. I feel like I started in Chicago with the Bears and George Halas, and I came back and did what I wanted to and lived up to his legacy. I'm not sure the Old Man could appreciate the significance of what him trusting me meant to me. Maybe he saw that I was a lot like him. That sounds funny even saying it. He was probably more serious than I was. I messed around a little, you know.

But that Super Bowl XX win stands alone in Chicago history. An ass-kicking. Pure and simple. It's like what columnist Bob Verdi wrote: "The New England Patriots were lucky to escape with their Boston accents intact."

Me, I thought somebody just invented this giant merry-go-round, and we were getting on, and we were going to ride forever. And it would be fun.

Then it all sort of ended. We continued for a while, but Buddy left to coach Philadelphia and jealousies came into play, and Wilbur Marshall went to Washington, and McMahon got hurt, and people said I did too many commercials and on and on. I've heard it all.

But I didn't change as a coach. I couldn't. It's my essence. The people who say outside stuff interfered with my drive are full of crap. I'm an emotional person. I get wrapped up in things. And I wanted this to go on and on. But it didn't, and no Bears team has ever gotten back to the Super Bowl. Think about it—of the two teams who played on that January 26, 20 years ago, one, the loser, the one that got crushed, has been back four times and won the game three times. And the other? Well, you know.

It's hard to take. There are a lot of reasons why it's happened, and I could tell you what I think and why I think it. I could tell you a lot of stuff. But that's for another day.

Besides, I don't get mad at things any more. Not things I can't control. Not life. Really, I don't. I only get mad at cab drivers now and then.

Because they're idiots.

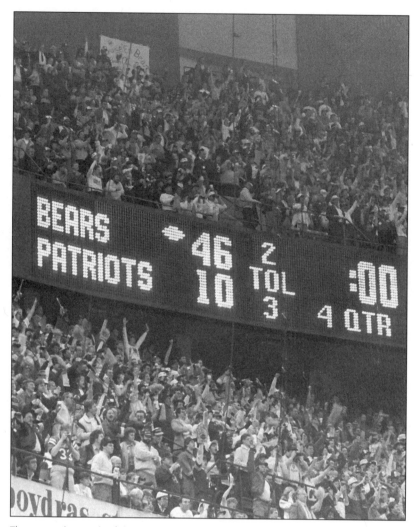

There it is—the peak of the mountain. *Photo by Vernon J. Biever*

AFTERWORD

After finishing my last reading of this book, I shut down my laptop, leaned back in my chair, stretched these creaky knees, and reflected on the Super Bowl Bears. Ah, yes, what a time it was. The magic came and left so quickly it seems maybe it never was here. But it was. Wasn't it?

Take my own roof. In 1986 workmen were doing some repairs up there—seems somebody was always hammering above—and I had a brainstorm: What if I put a sign there? The roof itself was very steep, too steep to stand on, but a worker had a roof ladder, the kind of ladder that has a piece that hooks over the peak and lays flat against the shingles. Before dusk I got a bucket of white house paint and a brush from the garage, climbed a regular ladder to the roof, clambered onto the roof ladder and sat there, looking out at the deserted Bears practice field and Halas Hall.

From the players' vantage point, my black roof would be a billboard staring them in the face, a "SEE ROCK CITY" barn side along a Tennessee highway. I carefully pried off the lid of the gallon can and began to paint. I was bubbling with Super Bowl giddiness, like all Bears fans, and this is what I painted: "46-10."

I didn't hear much from folks for a while—you had to be on the field to really notice, but from there it was like a neon sign in your eyeballs—until a year later Ditka saw me at practice and said, "Could you get that damn score off your roof? We haven't done crap."

He was mad because the Bears had lost the 1986 NFC playoff game to the Washington Redskins, and the Super Bowl score was a sharp stick in his side. It took a while, but I located the roof ladder again, maybe I called the worker who owned it, and I went back up on the roof. I painted a line through the 46-10 and painted, directly above it: "13-27," the losing score of that Redskins game. Another year went by, and the Bears lost in the playoffs again. To the Redskins.

"Dammit!" Ditka said this time. "Get those scores off your roof! They're killing me!"

But here was the problem. The roof ladder was gone, the workmen were long gone, and I wasn't interested in climbing onto those black shingles again, by any means. I could see myself tumbling off, being impaled on the fence below, ending a brief career with a bad obituary headline.

"Coach, I'm sorry, I can't get out there," I said. "But you can do whatever you want."

Time went by. One day I heard a whirring noise, a bump on the roof. I went onto my deck. The Bears' cherry-picker, the crane-like contraption from which cameraman Mitch Friedman filmed practice, had been driven to the edge of Bears territory, tilted forward, and now somebody was painting my roof with a long roller and black paint. The score was gone.

After a decade the numerals started to creep out. Then, a couple years back, we were hit by a bad hailstorm, the insurance company replaced my entire roof, and that was that.

What remains are the memories, the former players, and the coach—Ditka. If that 1985 season had all of the elements of the mythological journey—the leader with an outsized goal, the banding together, the trek, the battles, the temporary failure (Miami), the wise old adviser (Landry), the internal strife (Buddy), the redemption, the goal achieved, the uncertainty after success—Ditka has become the embodiment of the adventure. He could have become a clown, a caricature, even a nobody. But he stays in the public eye, being wise, being funny, being angry, being absurd, making contradictions, doing such things as saying he's running for U.S. Senator, making a movie, appearing on radio and TV, selling an erectile dysfunction drug, even coaching the woeful New Orleans Saints for a spell. "It's funny," he told me of that miscalculation, "but we played the Super Bowl in New Orleans, and because of that I thought somehow I could make it Chicago down there." Ricky Williams was going to be Ditka's new Walter Payton. Wrong.

Now people genuinely like old No. 89. His V-hairdo and mustache are not just trademarks, they're fun. Folks revere Ditka because he personifies things seemingly lost—guy-dom, the era before political correctness, old-time nasty football. But they also revere him because they can tell somewhere inside that huge, snarling carcass is a soft touch, a great big beating heart.

"I eat quitters for breakfast and spit out the bones!" Ditka bellows in *Kicking and Screaming*. But he's winking the whole time.

Yet he twitches with unfulfilled want. It's as though he's the biggest toddler in the world. It's like he was built with attack mode only and a dial that goes to 12. He fidgets, he plays solitaire, he grumbles to himself, he plays golf in the wind, snow, sleet. Sharks rest more than he does. You look at Iron Mike, and you know what he should be doing forever is catching a pass across the short middle, seeking a collision with the tough guy linebackers and maybe a couple safeties, if they want some.

It was fitting that we spent so much time in his cigar bar. "If people don't like smoke, they don't have to come," he'd say, firing up a stogie. It's perfect, because public smoking is darned near as vanished as the dodo. I never saw a dodo, but I miss those birds.

I think of Ditka's comments about Grabowskis and Smiths. Doug Smith, the Los Angeles Rams Pro Bowl center in 1985, told me back then, "My name's been Smith all along, and I never associated it with white collar or conformity. I mean, they're the ones making videos. We could make a video and there would be 50 sales—to our families."

He was right. The Bears were all kinds of things. Ditka himself was the Grabowski. And part of a Grabowski's essence is being restless, always slightly teed-off, ever the self-perceived underdog. Ditka can make a comment, then later reverse himself, then criss-cross it all like a foaming speedboat. Confront him with the wavy contradictions, and he'll solve everything by spouting, "Well, you can kiss my ass!"

Diana Ditka has seen it all. "Mike is just so honest," she says. And honestly, aren't we all contradictions like Mike? Isn't that the appeal? No matter how deep-thinking we get, don't we invariably come back to the caveman principal regarding life's ambiguities: kick its ass before it kicks yours?

My 14-year-old son and two buddies were at our kitchen table the other night, watching the tube. I said to them, apropos of nothing, "So the entire continent of Europe takes on 11 mini-Ditkas in a game of football. Who wins?"

"Easy, Mr. Telander," said one boy. "The mini-Ditkas."

"By how much?"

"Two hundred thirty-seven to nothing."

"Correct," I said.

I recalled more *Saturday Night Live* logic.

"Ditka and God are sitting at a bar," I said. "What are they talking about?"

"Trick question!" the boys shouted in unison.

"Why?" I asked.

"Ditka *is* God!"

Oh, whatever he is, he's a character. That's for sure. And sometimes characters are more than entertainment.

They're mini-treasures.

—RICK TELANDER
AUGUST 2005

INDEX

G

H